COSMIC
REVELATION

COSMIC
REVELATION

CHANNELED BY
ANN VALENTIN AND VIRGINIA ESSENE

 S.E.E. Publishing Company, Santa Clara, California USA

ISBN #0-937147-02-8
Library of Congress Catalog Card Number: 87-060936

Spiritual Education Endeavors
Publishing Company
1556 Halford Avenue, #288
Santa Clara, CA 95051
USA

First Printing June 1987

DEDICATION

This book is dedicated to God—the original Creator of all life, who made everything possible by manifesting cosmic energy and then birthing forth those twin creations, the Gold and Silver Rays.

It is also dedicated to those first-born creations, the Gold and Silver Rays, who bring us closer to the true reality of spiritual knowing and remembrance.

Most particularly it is dedicated to the great Silver Ray and the Supreme Council of Creation who cared enough to design the loveliest planet in our entire Universe so we dwellers of Earth could joyfully experience the glorious undeniable proof that God's power exists.

Then we wish to dedicate this book to each personality and soul upon planet Earth who dares to be open-minded about the Silver Ray's information, difficult as this may be for some. May your willingness, courage, and love bring a widespread change in human consciousness that frees us for our next great cosmic shift. Because of those like you, humanity will bond in spiritual power and purpose, and will make *preservation of all life and peace on Earth* a final accomplishment.

Thank you for all that you are and the actions you take for peace.

ACKNOWLEDGMENTS

Loving appreciation is given to Marijke Hoefnagels for her many hours of dedicated labor in the preparation of this manuscript ... to Bob Berkebile for the book's illustrations which were difficult to express on paper ... to John Willis for his assistance with Share Foundation ... to Elizabeth for her loving, cheerful ways, support, and many hours of help ... to Ruth and John who kept things going smoothly at the office ... and to the many Love Corps networkers for their encouragement and support during the process of completing this unusual book.

Deep gratitude, sincere appreciation, and loving recognition go to Blazena Muller for her lifelong dedication to the Christ Consciousness and Silver Ray energies ... and for her personal support to the Share Foundation.

* * * * * * * * * * * * * * * *

Most especially I—Virginia Essene—wish to thank Ann Valentin, my "powercell" partner who channels the Silver Ray energy, for her personal dedication to this great one and to our mutual purpose to God. Without her willingness to allow the Silver Ray's messages to be brought forth through her, there could not have been material for me to organize, edit, and present to the world in book form. Please excuse any errors.

And I—Ann Valentin—state that Virginia has again demonstrated her dedication through the many, many hours of work put into the completion of this book. Without her efforts it would not have such high quality. This truly seems a place where saying "thank you" is not enough. Nonetheless, with deepest appreciation and affection I say "thank you"!

My personal thanks to Lisa and David for their love, support, and understanding.

* * * * * * * * * * * * * * * * *

Finally, we both give soul-felt appreciation to the Silver and Gold Rays, and all those connected with these great creators, for their present efforts to awaken a sleeping humanity. How can we earth dwellers ever truly acknowledge the Great Rays and those 5 million light beings who give their efforts to help raise us back into true spiritual clarity?

Our words of gratitude to them may seem insufficient to us, but we trust that our deepest appreciation is already known and accepted in those realms where creation begins and is sustained eternally.

Of course, humanity's achievement of peace will be the most eloquent "thank you" of all.

PREFACE

Many times upon completion of a journey you review events and are amazed at how quickly time passed and what has occurred.

So it is with a single life experience or many. Hundreds, thousands, or millions of years may have passed historically, but in *reality* these are only happenings in the experience of a soul's eternal existence.

Therefore, we will endeavor through this book's information to give you a fuller understanding of the realities of life so that the spiritual aspect of you can be more in harmony with your physical body existence.

You are much greater than you know. You are unique, important, a thread in a tapestry, a vital piece in a puzzle of divine origin. All of these statements are true. For behold, each of you is a dearly beloved child, a child of the Universe, a child of the Creators. You are a precious entity, hence, that which you call "parent" cares about you. Many of you speak about God as the Father. This is acceptable, for it gives you a sense of security, a sense of a higher being with more power and authority watching over you, guiding you, caring about your welfare.

Then let this higher power now sustain you during this

period on your planet called the Time of Awakening, in which we bring a higher energy to the planet. During this time you face the *possibility* of major earth changes occurring due to human activities. Within these possible physical changes there will also be major emotional cleansings in each personality because we bring higher energy to the planet. These accelerated energy vibrations will affect each person on a cellular level and on a deep emotional and spiritual level. Many will not understand the changes they feel, but all living things will feel these stimulants knowingly or unknowingly. Be wise! Become consciously involved in this time of change. This new energy, which began August 1, 1985, is intended to lift you into the higher plane of peace and assure a positive outcome for your planet, C-ton (pronounced see-tawn). In the highest realm the accurate name of your planet is C-ton.

Some of the information in this publication will not be new. You may have read it before, heard it in your meditations, or learned it from those channels who bring information of this immediate hour to your attention. Perhaps the contents will only confirm what you have already felt or understood in your innermost thoughts—information known to your soul or higher self.

Much of the information I share will be totally new! I ask that you do not reject any data on first reading but that you ponder it and see if you can give its message serious consideration. Within the information is the element of education at the *highest* spiritual level. You Earth dwellers are becoming aware that some of you originally came from someplace else, and during this Time of Awakening it is possible that a yearning to leave this planet and its woes may surface. But your soul will urge you to stay and resolve the negative conditions that you see. Now is the moment to help, even if you feel tempted to flee.

The reason you feel an urgency to improve Earth's conditions is because it was your soul's choice to come and do just that! The very purpose of your existence here is to be of assistance to this planet. It was for this reason you came, individually and collectively. You came to make a difference. This feeling is part of your underlying soul commitment to serve and, if followed, will allow you to benefit from the many physical, emotional, and spiritual changes that are to happen. In this time lies the opportunity to achieve mastery, to experience forgiveness for all negative past life actions, and to continue your journey to the higher realms, homeward bound.

When you look at the stars and the nighttime sky, you may feel a longing to return home. You may be aware of your separation from your former home in the Universe. We know of the yearning of your heart and soul, and we are here to help. Unite now with your spiritual family on the Earth plane, and with your unseen family of light, too. These unseen forces are here with the blessings and endowment of energies from the God force itself. Let us rejoice as we symbolically reach out our arms to comfort, assist, and guide you on your journey through the stars.

Now let us extend your personal knowledge and correct humanity's perception by uncovering some information lost in the portals of time.

The Silver Ray

TABLE OF CONTENTS

NOTE TO READERS

In God all things are genuinely ONE, so beings who come from high states of consciousness often express this by the language of "we," "us," and "ours"—rather than "I," "me," and "mine."

Consequently, when these high energies communicate with us on Earth, "we" is frequently used, even though one distinctive energy may be thinking and communicating. Please be aware of this as you read <u>Cosmic Revelation</u>, channeled to humanity primarily by the Silver Ray. There will be some occasions, however, when the word "I" is utilized by an individual communicator.

Also please understand that the use of "he" or "his" does not exclude the feminine "she" and "hers." These spiritual beings and rays are androgynous. We ask you to accept the English language limitation in this matter as we say "he" or "his," and extend it to mean both female and male. *There is no lessening of the female quality or nature intended!*

The materials not written by the Silver Ray, such as a chapter by Jesus or comments by the Gold Ray, are clearly marked.

Welcome, then, from the very throne of existence, a simplified message for all who desire to know the actual workings of creation with deeper reverence and clarity.

Chapter 1

New Truths for a Time of Awakening

If you could imagine yourself on another plane of existence without physical limitations and restrictive personality patterns, for a time, and look down upon planet Earth, you would have a much different view and an immense insight. This would bring into perspective the great horror of human hatred, violence, and spiritual unconsciousness, resulting in severe and chronic planetary abuse.

You would clearly see what has happened to the once most beautiful planet in your universe, the human disdain for animals and plants brought here for you to care for. You would recognize the lunacy of military weapons and realize the probability of destruction for Earth and space life unfortunate enough to be nearby.

You would probably be so appalled that you would want to reverse the situation immediately, because Earth's insane activities could trigger an energy explosion to wreak havoc with your own residence. What neighbor lives next to a burning house without fear? Without calling for assistance to put out the blaze? Obviously such a fire must be quenched or it will spread unchecked! And so a galactic fire alarm is sounded.

Two responses follow immediately. The first is a call for help to protect all in the fire's path. The second is concern for those insane ones producing this danger.

The first call alerts all beings in various levels of authority, in many realms of physical and spiritual density, to find short-term solutions to the emergency. The space craft called UFO's that appeared after World War II sought these short-term solutions. They observed and advised their commanders about the gravity of the situation. Because the Earth is a free will planet, as a gift of the Silver Ray, and an ancient charter prohibits direct galactic intervention without consultation from the Creators, they watched and waited. But at the highest level in the Omniverse the Great Rays became apprised of the situation, and as the underground hydrogen explosions continue, there is deepening concern about the experimental station C-ton, presently known as Earth.

Now a further concern surfaces. Who will volunteer to help change this critical situation? Millions of assistants are needed for a massive "awaken-the-Earth" team. If this final attempt for peace fails, the sleeping souls will not achieve the growth required for spiritual mastery. Then only a few will go forward in the light. You ponder such a fate, perhaps recalling your own soul's journey through the darkness of a third dimensional experience.

Knowing those who have started the fire could be physically destroyed and spiritually retarded, would you ignore their plight and the danger they represent? What would you do? Would your spiritual caring and compassion bring you forward to help?

Imagine others like yourself watching this spectacle, also. Some of them are graduated caretakers of Earth who clearly see that the job isn't finished. Others have done such unloving things in their lives that they owe Earth and humanity restitution or the repayment of negative karma.

Whichever reason was yours, family of mine, if you are

reading this book, you *were* out of the physical body on another reality level, and you *did* return for this great rescue mission.

Can you remember any of this story?

You were there! And now you are here with a veil that we wish to remove because the negative thoughts of Earth are captivating and overpowering. Truly, this is your hour of awakening as we pour the vibrations of our refined energies to refresh you, to stir your soul, and to bring you into the light.

We inform you for three reasons. First, because we care about you. You see, you are a created being of energy that was given life eons ago. Even though many upon Earth have forgotten God and executed deeds that fill your history books with horror, they too may be redeemed by helping the planet at this critical time. Those in higher authority could have refused forgiveness to tarnished souls, but the decision was made to offer all souls one last chance to preserve life upon this planet. Yes, the choice was made to forgive, even when the souls have repeatedly created havoc.

I say once again that we care about you! This is your proof: forgiveness; one more chance. This is the moment of decision for all souls who must not repeat previous injustices and misdeeds. To do so automatically precludes any return to Earth during its Thousand Years of Peace. But you have heard this thought before. Is it not said that you should go and sin no more? Meaning to stop the *negative* and begin the *positive* behavior.

Secondly, these truths are shared so you may take advantage of the new energies brought to this planet by the great Silver Ray. This is an unprecedented moment in human experience. This Ray is the creator of your planet and your individual soul. This powerful one calls you to bring your individual ray—the soul—its spiritual transfusion with the energy of the rainbow spectrum. The Silver Ray made the colors and birthed many high beings and subrays, to continue the process of creation as the many universes were made and extended.

This story of the Rays is not known to you of Earth at all, but we present it now at the request of the many who are awakening and wondering who they are and why they are here. Even the birds and animals feel your Great Rays' presence and drink deeply of the unfolding consciousness they stimulate. You have had the Gold Ray, or Christ Light, about 7 million years, but it is now greatly amplified. The one called Silver Ray, twin to the Gold, is a magnificent benefactor! The Silver Ray is the maker of moonlight, originator of the rainbow, and healer of your subconscious mind and soul.

Finally, you are being told these secret truths so you will take action for peace. The Earth is at a critical junction because of your misuse of atomic, nuclear, and hydrogen materials. This dangerous situation needs your attention, your commitment, and your efforts. We would not speak this way if it were not important. Hydrogen is an elemental building block of the energy design in your Universe. Detonating it can destroy the fabric of space, as well as cause the Earth's interior demolition. Since hydrogen is part of the fabric of space, once detonated it would be similar to your cancerous growths. It would not stop expanding, but would continue to destroy, destroy, destroy. Its spread would be limitless because all of what you call space contains hydrogen. Since water is two parts hydrogen to one part oxygen, you could destroy this, also. It could affect everything eventually. I can assure you that the great Silver Ray would not be attending this tiny place in the outskirts of your small galaxy if it were not *imperative*. I repeat the word imperative for emphasis. You are caretakers of all forms of life on Earth, caretakers of the planet itself. And you must help bring peace to C-ton now.

Since the release of New Teachings for an Awakening Humanity and other recently channeled messages, the higher realms have pondered whether humanity is ready to know the truth of its actual origins, including an explanation of what God is and is not. We do not desire to create chasms among the various religions, philosophies, institutions and belief systems so strongly entrenched in the recent history of the planet, but rather to *unite* them into a body of souls concerned about peace. Yet there is a risk involved here which we choose to take.

We have released much metaphysical information during the last hundred years in England and America, where Theosophy, the various "mystery" schools, the Alice Bailey materials, the Edgar Cayce books, the healing churches, the Urantia Book, A Course in Miracles, and many other inspirational books and music have done much to spur the awareness of human consciousness in your western cultures. Even teachers from the eastern lands have come to share their knowledge. Yet due to the threat of hydrogen and nuclear extinction, these groups *must come together* in spite of apparent separativeness. It is time to link and to create larger and larger light units. It is for this reason you are all here together. Yes, you had past relationships that may bring attachment to one soul personage or body of knowledge, but we are superseding all of it now with the Great Rays' intervention. These powers are fueling the many spiritual teachers and their teachings, but more urgently, they birth your souls into a greater reality or spiritual evolution than you can imagine. Honor the past but do not be limited by it. Come into the *present!* Only it holds your key to Earth's reclamation.

The messages of the Lords of Light, the Archangels, the subangelic realms, the spiritual masters, the ascended ones, and those who have learned peace are being amplified by these

Great Rays now, and so the combined support of all people of good will, especially those called light workers, is critical.

If not for the underground hydrogen explosions and the atomic and nuclear materials being used in weaponry and other unsafe purposes, your present spiritual teachers and guides would have continued their work uninterrupted. But with the acceleration of possible technological disaster—being re-lived from former Atlantean days—immediate action had to be taken. Why? Because the addition of the spiritual discernment/cosmic wisdom factor to the blue ray of human intellect is not being used by enough scientists and military people today. Because the secrets of the tools of destruction are once again in the hands of the heartless ones, many of whom apparently will not learn the lesson of love or caring for the lifeforms on Earth. They are repeating the horrendous weapons and tactics of their Atlantean power-hungry days. And the quiet majority ignores or refuses its responsibility in this crucial matter. We now call both of these groups to demonstrate love and wisdom.

Understand, we do not ask anyone to forget the wonderful work that the past spiritual teachers have brought to the Earth. They were, and are, all necessary with their efforts and integrity of service. Most still work diligently on behalf of Earth to teach you moral lessons. But frankly, the intervention that had to happen has begun. The first two energies born of God, the Gold and Silver Rays, have joined with their unimaginable powers to stop the fearsome trend toward destruction. Consequently you have a sudden interjection of these great creator energies to awaken humanity to its peril, and all of heaven stands in astonishment. Never before has such a thing happened!

Because of an intergalactic charter which prohibits even a free will planet from being self-destructive, since its aftermath would obviously harm others living in the womb of God's cosmic energy, the Parent-of-all has now reminded Earth to establish peace *at once.*

In <u>Secret Truths for Teens and Twenties</u> the horrendous effect of the planet Maldek's self-demolition by satanic scientists was cited as the reason this charter was instigated. Even as you have Earth agreements, this is a God-approved contract and must not be violated by you! Your hydrogen testing and nuclear weapons already represent a greater threat than Maldek did.

This intervention in Earth's affairs, known and approved of by the very energy of God, began on August 1, 1985. It was increased on November 17, 1986, when God and the Great Rays concluded that a sufficient core of peace energy had been established by committed light workers and some other stirring ones who seemed to have started their awakening process. The original 18 months were extended for an additional two years in an even more accelerated and intense fashion. This gift continues until November, 1988's evaluation time. Because this intensified support is an actual change in energy vibration, expressing as *time awareness*, I will outline its possible effects on you and for the planet at large.

This basic energy shift in the quality or lightness of the Earth's vibration affects everything, just as the rays of the Sun and Moon affect all life. Your personal perception of time may be individual, but this effect will go beyond that to the entire planet. The acceleration of time will be a *planetary* reality. Now you cannot save time for tomorrow. This is the great equalizer. You all have just 24 hours in one day. How you use that time is individual, but as you notice time's acceleration the activities that usually would have taken a day to accomplish may take about 20 percent longer by November, 1987. Therefore, you have to work with the *quality* of your time; you must carefully prioritize your values and use time for peaceful purposes. More than ever, *TIME IS YOUR EXISTENCE!* even though in our reality, time does not exist.

Time is one of three measurements in your present world so your perceptions are limited by these definitions of time, space, and motion. But we are changing you to a fourth dimension where time vanishes and we note life by its events or happenings, rhythms and cycles, etc. In an interesting way, what you call "time" is vanishing.

Have you noticed lately that your experience of time is even now becoming more fleeting and difficult to manage than before?

If you are eating lightly—primarily vital, living foods—and are getting enough exercise and rest, you will make this transition more easily. Enjoy the benefits of daily meditation during this time, and join with your spiritual friends weekly to share this exhilarating new energy. From it you can more easily manifest the peace so desperately required. Some of your scientists think that these cosmic leaps in consciousness are accomplished by humanity itself, but this is not so. It is the energy of the higher dimensions that triggers this evolution and enables life to continue its progress constructively. We feed you with a higher quality of energy.

Although you are not creating the energy shift, appreciate this gift of increased vibration, and take credit for wisely utilizing it. Do not suppose you are capable of playing God, although you may be assured that God is a part of you. Your soul is a constellation of energy rays or beams to guide your physical body during your experience here. You are not true creators of matter and lifeforms, but you are using God's cosmic power to manifest peace for yourself, groups, and now an entire planet.

You have been given "dominion" as a species, so let me

clarify what we mean this to be. Although your scriptures use the word dominion, this has not been understood correctly. Humanity was placed in charge of the *welfare* of other beings placed here by the Silver Ray, not in a position of *rulership*. Hence, you are all responsible to see that the other lifeforms, soul-filled or soulless, continue in healthy existence. Dominion is to be interpreted as caring for created matter and all lifeforms present here and beyond.

Humankind can discern, decide, progress, or regress in the movement of life's energies. You have free will, but the evolutionary pattern of the planet is forward motion and creative response to life. It is our hope and endeavor that humankind will move forward also. This movement evolves you toward the Time of Radiance very quickly now, bringing the planet itself *back* to the high level it once had. We are raising the human form *back* to its high design and embodiment of the God force energy. Your dominion or caretaking role in this is cooperation and a respectful *awareness* of the universe and its laws. No Earth dwellers may go out into the universe and try to change or rule other areas of space in any way or manner. A visitor you may be, but only that.

However, taking the environment of Earth into the outer regions is allowed if no weapons are carried in your vehicles. This permission to visit is granted only so you can acquire a perspective of other regions. You may *not harm* any created thing, be it a planet, star, or the *fabric of space* itself. There are to be no accidents, mistakes, or misjudgments that will have far-reaching negative effects. Earth is your dominion, then. If you accomplish *this* responsibility you may officially graduate to greater cosmic opportunities.

What *can* occur, if you are attentive in these two years to our increased spiritual assistance, is that your brain will begin to expand. Those vibrations the Great Rays bring will stimulate your intellectual capabilities. You have been using only a tiny percent of that ingeniously designed brain to survive and cope with life. As in other Renaissance periods, this one will foster immense creativity, but of a much *higher* order. We hope that this energy change will help humanity focus on peaceful pursuits in personal, group, and planetary ways.

Since you have been given two additional years to use this energy, you will notice several things. One, your personality may seem to be "out of control" somehow. And yet you should have a greater sense of happiness and joy as you are saturated in soul attunement by our God force intervention. Join with your spiritual friends to improve the planet and receive new ideas about making the Earth a better place.

We hope that you will use this improved creativity to make immense positive strides in all areas. Especially focus on the Earth as a healthier place to be! Solve a myriad of practical problems, like identifying the most vital food sources and obliterating poverty and hunger. Use the new vibration to resolve ways of thinking about war and violence, and concentrate on peaceful living. It can be a bright, vibrant time for individuals, families, and groups—the whole planet and all its lifeforms!

As you welcome this new time and its changes, you will be able to consciously utilize our gift to its fullest. Those who resist or ignore the feelings and information will likely fall behind as the energy vibrations increase and time races along like an accelerating vehicle.

Your Earth is a vehicle—your space vehicle. As it rotates along its course of solar travel, many changes will likely bring you closer to your higher consciousness and memory of God. This planet is a created thing. It is matter and energy as you are. Enjoy your ride through space and your elevated opportunity now for greater love and peace. We come to offer you caring, to give you an opportunity for self-mastery, and to bring Earth's urgent situation to your attention.

We have many plans for lessons and experiences in the coming years, depending upon the rapidity with which you can learn and implement peace. Let the Silver Ray's energies grant you the chance to make a genuine difference in the way your world works. You are children of the Great Rays. You are energy. What you do with it rests now in your hands and with those who are the caregivers, the caretakers, the love bringers.

There are 5 million invisible forces here to help you, wanting to call you into an awakened state! There has *never* been such an armada of light on Earth. If you have any previous misdeeds or negative karma, this is the time to release it by completing your soul's mission.

You are an evolving creation now supported by our intensified two-year commitment of help. This offer is given with care and concern. Please accept it in the same mood and accomplish that which your soul undertook before you came here this lifetime. If you and we are joined in the one great bond of love and wisdom, life will be all that was intended in the beginning, before time was.

Now I will speak two minutes to the soul within each of you, if you will grow still and picture a gold and silver radiance around you.

I begin by saying: Old soul, stirring in remembrance of its goal chosen outside of time, do you not remember that you are needed here and are this day called forth? Old soul, if you complete that which you came to do, believe that the grace, or removal of negative imbalances in your experience, will be granted forever. Old soul, you will have only three callings to agree to fulfill your particular part in preserving life on Earth. Know that at the review following this life, all souls must have demonstrated peace to receive cosmic advancement. You have

11

now received your *first calling* of those three granted, so if you are not already "about your father's business," ponder this calling well.

I ask you to create one picture, now, in your mind, old soul. Please see Earth from space as the astronauts who travel there have shown you. See that you are one planet, but you have other solar system relationships. Respect them, and picture your planet healed of violence and war for their sake and yours. Visualize this wonderful, vibrant Earth with humanity awakened, interacting peacefully with all of life: plants, animals, gems and minerals, creatures of the sea, and birds of the air. Hold this vision. Become this vision! You can create it by mutual agreement and action.

Yes, old soul, in this shining moment we will take the planet and her occupants to a timeless consciousness that sings God's celestial melody and glows with showers of pure gold and silver, dancing in the midnight sky of cosmic energy.

Then give your gift of caring, old soul, so it can take you home again where you have longed to be. And where we expectantly await your return into the foreverness beyond time.

AMEN

Christ Jesus

Chapter II

You and Creation

Creation is power that has been demonstrated. You must grasp what creation truly is and how it works to successfully create peace. Since creation is manifested energy, peace must be created. This simple statement is paramount. Although you have only limited creative power in your present responsibility as a caretaker, you must employ all this power to bring peace into reality. Another word for power is spirit. The Holy Spirit is holy power. No matter what is created with it, you can take the energy apart and go into all of its apparent divisions or levels so that at the end you discover a molecule, atom, and even smaller particles, *connected to everything else.* All things and events have innumerable levels and connections. Creation always involves the whole and its parts in relationship.

In perceiving matter and existence, look at, in, beyond, above, below, and through that which you think you see. Realize that, if you do not physically see the *energy*, your perception is limiting your idea of reality. Much has been written to tell you that your life is an illusion. Take no offense at this! One day you will see that the energy we speak of has been there all along. But realize that this energy eases your way through your temporary, blind existence and permits release from what you call suffering.

Nothing that happens on your Earth on a non-spiritual energy level is **real.** When you perceive that you are suffering, know that it can be lived through and it will pass. It is mobile, not stationary or solid or permanent. Yes, you experience a pain. But each thing changes, moment to moment, even in the physical body. Our purpose is to free you from the illusion of your beliefs about life, from yesterday and its apparent finality. We encourage you to be in the present moment where the opportunity of seeing and using positive, cosmic energy is truly your salvation, if you can but grasp it.

Throughout your planet, people are beginning to have dreams, visions, or vague remembrances of a time long ago when they existed as light beings without a dense physical body. Now many are silent about this awareness because they are afraid of others' reactions to these feelings. The remembrance is like a distant dream, not quite clear and yet defined enough to cause discomfort, or even pain, in the memory.

The early existence of some souls on this planet was as a non-physical being of a light molecular vibration. For these souls, a personal nagging may go on from the soul level to the personality consciousness.

Why not accept that this is the truth of you, if you sense it, and explore the significance of your life on Earth today? Many do not speak about it, feeling that something is wrong with them—that they are peculiar or even crazy. Unfortunately, when they finally risk sharing these feelings, there may not be another accepting person to listen, to agree, to confirm. Humans need to feel safe in sharing that there is more to them than one body, one lifetime, one planetary experience. We assure you, lifetimes have been spent when speaking openly has brought miserable results and there may be hesitancy to be outspoken. In voicing these thoughts, then, humans want acceptance and explanation of their experience. It is this we bring.

14

You might ask, where did these first non-physical beings on Earth come from? Who were those energies who lived elsewhere in the galaxy?

To begin this discussion, please understand that your planet, which we call C-ton, is the most beautiful planet in this 12th Universe. It is the most unique because of its *variety*. It has more lifeforms than any other planet, more beauty per square inch than places previously created. Nowhere else can you find the many rocks, gems and minerals, the plants and trees, the abundant animal life, and the many moving creations of air and sea. Never has a place been so carefully planned, so generously given total attention to variety of color, form, and interrelationships of all living things. In flowers alone, the artistry and beauty and variety are voluminous. How many trees exist? How many foods have we provided? In fruit alone, this planet has more choice than was ever before created on a single site. *To be unaware of this is to miss the entire purpose of the planet.* Truly Earth is the Garden of Eden. After millions of years of planning and creating, we finally birthed this wonderful, exciting, beautiful place into dense form, ready for habitation and caretaking. That sequence of events as briefly outlined in the holy book called the Bible is fairly accurate, although the time sequence lacks specificity, and the Great Rays of morning and night, the two first-born creations, are not clarified as being creators themselves, which they are.

In a more thorough explanation of how your planet C-ton was created, let me share this additional data regarding the groundwork necessary for the creation of such an exquisite place. The groundwork begins with the determination of where to place a planet. Decisions must be made as to the appropriateness of putting a physical form of matter in a specified space. Then the size of that matter must be planned. The content or structure of the matter is defined. Will it be a single star? A star cluster? A single planet? What is desired and why?

If it is to be a single planet, we decide what its purpose is to be and what size would best accomplish its use. But creation is not always a purely logical decision, as you might think. It is often joyfulness expressing the desire for beauty or uniqueness—something different from what has gone before. Creation can be purely playful in its intention.

Let me say more about this playful spirit in relation to C-ton. In the 12th Universe there was a large void. Here I, the Silver Ray, decided to make a small planet—an experimental one of great beauty and variety. I say "I" because that which you call God has empowered into life, in its image, two Great Rays. One is gold and one silver. Both of these creations, as direct offspring of the First Cause, can create matter and energy lifeforms.

The Bible says that God issued the Word. Another meaning of the Word would be beams of energy or winds of cosmic power, emanating creative intention. The Gold and Silver Rays are God in expression outside of itself. Into the womb of life that God had prepared, which we shall call *Cosmic* energy, that immense force also sent forth part of itself as two great energy rays for creative purposes. We, the Gold and Silver Rays, were that Word made manifest—"the morning and the night." It is we who have continued to create in God's name since that immaculate conception long ago.

In the very beginning we did not know our powers or what we were to do, odd as that may sound. This awareness came gradually and with experience. We worked together in the early universes and then, by agreement, took areas of specialization. The Gold Ray became a paramount bringer of universal laws and respect for God. The Silver Ray continued the

16

creative process of bringing life into form, even as an artist paints or a musician composes. In this way we are often referred to as male and female, but we are, in fact, both equally powerful and capable of all things. This is more than androgyny as you know that definition. It is the combined totality of all that God chose to express of itself. We Rays are the thrust or impulse of creative activity. We are the manifestors of life through our Parent. Through us life has spread.

Now let me say more about creation in relation to the 12th Universe and your own planet. I, the Silver Ray, with help from those ten subrays that I birthed out of myself, and the super beings called the Lords of Light who were also my creations, made the 12th Universe. Since this Universe had a large void, I decided to make a very beautiful planet called C-ton. It was what you would call an experimental station.

The designation of this new planet required that a number of souls or beings, created from the Silver Ray, assist in the work that constantly goes on in creating matter. My Supreme Council of Creation discussed and clarified tasks called for by the original design requirements much as an architectural group would do on Earth. Thereafter, we needed souls to carry out the specific tasks of manifestation and sent out a call for volunteer caretakers.

Because of the very unusual free will experiment intended for your planet, I will clarify at some length the features that predominate and affect the outcome of your planet's future. For in your understanding of this planetary experiment, it is hoped you can more wisely care for the entire creation with spiritual discernment and responsibility.

One aspect of the creative design for C-ton was that the planet itself and every created thing upon its surface would be interdependent. That is, *no one lifeform could exist without the others.* This interdependency is not the usual pattern of

17

planetary life, so careful planning and effort for its fruition and maintenance were required. I repeat this point because it is at the core of your existence as a human living among other created forms. You need plants; they are your lifeline to oxygen, to breath. To believe otherwise is folly. You do not have the power to change or ignore this interdependency. Only your knowledge and commitment to its holistic nature can preserve the planet.

In the very beginning, the volunteer souls, or spiritual beings, were not living among the other forms upon the planet; you volunteers lived above the planet's surface as spiritual lifeforms, as caretakers. If you can truly grasp that you are still a caretaker with healing work to do for the planet, you can take your place as planetary saviors and can accept this task to be done. That is why I come to explain these things to you now. Your scriptures do not adequately state the particular reasons we created this planet. Thus you do foolish things. Your scriptures speak of dominion, but not about your particular *responsibilities* as caretakers under our aegis. We wish to reverse your pattern of destruction.

Your planet is a total, complete unit, a unified package of life that must relate to all portions of itself for survival. It is time for you to hear, to honor, and to support our creative design on C-ton. You did not make the planet, but you dwell here and must obey the universal laws in effect. Please listen well to that which I bring and utilize your wisdom in this critical hour for the safety of all concerned. Here on this experimental place you see why love and respect are so necessary. Without them what can the outcome be but death and destruction? Do you know that most planets have only three to seven elements upon them? But your planet is a jewel of variety and attractiveness! To it was added the most radical part of the experiment, free will. *For if there is variety, there must be free will to choose!* *It was this* **free will factor, intended for joy and appreciation,** *however, that has caused endless destruction* and with which we are urgently coping during this Time of Awakening.

For you and all lifeforms are made of the same 110 *primary* elements as the Earth. Copper, zinc, iron, gold, silver, nickel, uranium, plutonium, and the many other metals known to you, had to be chosen in the original composition of the planet to meet the size and weight requirements for gravitational pull conditions. Even those elements of the mineral kingdom below the ground and those creatures upon the surface are related.

Primarily we worked to create the planet as an entity that could be somewhat solid and yet maintain its orbital placement without mishap. This is no small feat, as I hope you and your Earth scientists appreciate. We continue to be surprised at the naivete of how you think all the worlds were created. If nothing else, I hope to change your awareness about the simplistic way you regard creation. Yes, God exists, but it is time to understand that the Parent works through its genealogical creations, and we through ours, to master the tasks of preparing physical universes that you take for granted. Some of you reading this material may remember, half-recall, or just imagine, other planets and their design, their characteristics and definitions. If you can do this, your comprehension of this information will be easier.

The chemistry of C-ton was to be quite unique with carbon-based planetary substance, an abundance of water, and an appreciable landmass. It would have an atmosphere on which the lifeforms would be dependent, a fact that is not usually the case.

We chose certain elements for C-ton because they contained aspects and movement that could help develop denser lifeforms that might be needed later. We chose carbon because it is

19

prevalent in this region of the universe and because of its blue-white color.

Another primary design factor was the immense variety of every type of species. Thus, not just one tree would be created, but hundreds of different kinds would populate the landmass, and they would each have their own healing powers. The evergreens would nurture and energize the planet itself. Redwood trees would have energies to heal the heart and throat areas of lifeforms. (Since "the fall," for example, even you humans are soothed there in the quiet outpouring of their heavenly therapy—majestic reminders of God's creative power.)

With each species having particular qualities to aid other living forms, the interdependency was established and must even now be maintained. But this great variety would also be interesting, joyful, and beautiful. If you have ever looked at the vast array of flowers, plants, trees, animals, birds, and sea creatures, you will feel a deep appreciation for our choices and designs. It is a garden, dwellers of C-ton. It truly is a garden, if you but knew some of the other planets and their design.

To recap the creation of C-ton, we began with an idea or intention. We decided to make a small planet in an unused part of space, totally different than anything else, and to give its caretakers free will. Then we researched what gases had drifted to that available area and determined if any solid matter or objects had gravitated to that vicinity.

In the beginning of our birth as Rays from God's awareness, we started *without* such materials in form and learned by experimentation. But we use such things when they are available. It was not easy to learn to bring forth all creation from within our God-nature. Suffice to say, by this time in the 12th Universe, I have had much practice in bringing many different creations into existence. Many of the prior planets are beautiful or unique or interesting, yet this small place is a work of art.

Know this, oh caretakers, and respect where you are, what you are. We must combine our energies to keep the planet and all life safe. I thank you for your assistance and dedication as a caretaker of C-ton.

Now I ask the Gold Ray to share his comments about this topic before I continue.

The Silver Ray

THE GOLD RAY'S MESSAGE

My experience of being created from the beingness of the great First Cause was one of awareness. I was conscious of God and myself and my twin. I was attached to my parent by an umbilical cord of pure energy and felt a deep communication beyond expression. If you could see me, there would be a golden stream of radiance a mile long and a half-mile across—greater than a million suns. In the quality of my essence was both positive and negative. I realized I would cease to exist eventually without my parent's energy flow, but there was no sense of danger. Before me was an additional awareness—an impression of immense spaciousness containing vitality but no matter. I knew that I was being encouraged to create something to fill that "void." It was like having a blank check or canvas, an opportunity to do whatever I might wish. After a time of simple experimentation, the Silver Ray and I worked together to create a planet and then a universe. We learned by doing, even as your soul does. In the 3rd Universe, however, I realized one of our rays would have to be a sustaining principle for God's laws and power, and I took this vital task upon myself.

Because of the Rebel Ray, which does not respect the Parent-of-All (and eventually went away to do some of his own creations), we perceived major difficulties in the creative process and organized our two energy focuses differently. We decided then not to destroy anything that had been created, even that one gone astray. We have not wished to be destructive, although we have that power.

After our decision not to destroy any life or let things die, I began upholding God's laws as one powerful focused *light,* while the Silver Ray continued to focus more on the creation of universes with lifeform creations. I have become more involved in the *principles* of Universal Law, or the mental and intellectual use of those aspects called will and power. The Silver Ray now uses the colors and energies of his essence for creation. I use my vibrations, or impulse, to energize existing creations for spiritual development and cooperation in and between various universes.

Now you must understand that about 7 million years ago upon this planet, when my Gold Ray energy perceived our spiritual volunteers languishing into negativity resulting in an actual reduction in the size of their energy bodies, action had to be taken. As a great plea went forth to God for help, I beamed my golden power toward the 12th Universe and embraced your planet Earth with this energy. Thus, any soul willing to remember its true origin and nature could be maintained.

This assistance to existing lifeforms is what brought my focus here to planet Earth after what your scriptures call the separation and "the fall." For, after the pain and sorrow of that small expedition's unsuccessful bout with the Rebel Ray's influence, there was a deep depression in the souls who remained upon Earth. It was my wish to support those souls and feed them hope. Thus, I focused my will and intention here that they should be encouraged and wish to continue living, to have soul existence. That is why the veil was drawn over their traumatic planetary experience and remembrance—so they would wish to continue. My vitality was needed because it is still the Gold Ray's energy that pulsates its support for remembrance of the Creator.

My Gold Ray sends you support and is now joined on Earth for the first time by the great Silver Ray. Although we both come from the First Cause and are equally empowered, we have nonetheless acquired, by agreement, slightly different frequencies. In this way the material worlds and all life can be maintained, even as new worlds of matter are being planned and formed by the Silver Ray, the Supreme Council, and the Lords of Light.

As the Gold Ray, it may be easier to equate me with electrical impulse, or *push*, while the Silver Ray's energy has a more nurturing aspect. Again I say to you that we are two energies equal in power—seemingly different—but harmoniously working together in the One. Only if it is the Creator's wish will we come again, side by side, as we were first thrust forth.

The appearance that our activities are separate and we therefore are different can be answered this way. We both have the qualities that you might call male and female in our nature, but we focus on one of these more than the other. God's nature in matter requires a balance, even as your own nature is coming to inner balance of these polarities. The Gold Ray may focus on having lifeforms stay within a framework of spiritual respect, but the Silver Ray certainly understands and expresses this, also.

I have been sending lower vibrational energies here for millions of years, having committed to this reclamation work, but the greatest thing happening upon your planet today is that the Silver Ray is focusing his energy and personal attention to join my own call. It is an unprecedented and unheard of event in the many universes. Can you be still a moment and realize that part of the combined essences of God have left other duties for considerable lengths of time to assist humanity? This is fantastic. Understand the importance of this great, unusual occurrence. The Rays are here to uplift an entire civilization, a planet, and the solar system and galaxy that is endangered by the violence you have bred here.

I beamed my own ray to Earth following that era of "the fall" to overcome the fear and misery of the events that had just happened and have kept the prospect of remembrance and redemption ever present to all souls. In the early days of those negative events the soul remembrance was painfully keen and vivid. For who would not be traumatized by the force of battle between the Rebel Ray and our own Blue Ray Master, Archangel Michael? Who would not weep when the Rebel Ray prevailed?

My strong energizing influence was needed to encourage energies to stay here for the completion of their original contract as Earth's caretakers.

My energy to instill courage and the will to live was appreciated by those who remained after the difficult times. However, that portion of energy which I focused here was only a low vibration, then, as my full power cannot safely be withdrawn from the other holy light universes.

After the souls' descent into density and their inability to return to the former high soul vibration, many great teaching souls came to your planet to bring you universal principles and awaken you to your true nature, origin, and earthly responsibilities. They have all used the power of my cosmic will and intention. The messages have persisted, but, sadly, few have listened during your past thousands of years.

The great teachers of *all major world religions* have been

fueled by the force and power of the Gold Ray. Your term "Christ Consciousness" or "Christ Light" means there is a universal understanding and respect for God and the laws which uphold creation. *My energy is the Christ Consciousness or Christ Light in this 12th Universe.* This is often just called light or love. "The Christ" usually means a world teacher of light and inspiration—a particular soul using the Gold Ray to improve the spiritual quality of all souls. It emphasizes love as a caring emotion or caring aspect of existence. Although you have had Christ Light teachers on Earth in the last 6,000 years your progress languishes. That is why I amplify my Gold Ray energy vibration in the ethers now.

Let me pause here to clarify an issue about which you of Earth constantly bicker—namely, who is the most important spiritual teacher and what religion is best. You are requested to unify, not be prideful in your relationships, for it is all very simple.

There is one God force, an energy. Realize it is the Power of Existence. It is the beginning of all, yet not the actual Creator of all that is in existence. It birthed two children called Rays. The Gold Ray represents God's authority, will, and power. It is this energy needed in material worlds to keep all life in cooperative alignment.

When spiritual teachers and advisors appear in a dimension like yours that has "time," they bring my influence and support. This is freely given, and whatever names are used in a myriad of languages, we still seek the same result. Your awareness of self as part of all life and your willingness to learn and grow responsibly as part of a huge cosmic family are the tenets we use. You, like us, are responsible for your deeds or creations. This responsibility is absolutely basic in a holy light universe.

How simple this message is and how complex your way of reviewing the truth and incorporating its loving behavior. Yet you will see the relationship of all these teachings, hopefully, and see the diverse parts as the true unity they really are. This unity is what consciousness confers and what enlightenment obtains.

These Earth teachers have had many names in your history books, yet they are essentially One mind expression, even in your limited perceptions. When you grasp and live this truth, you will be spiritually healed: your soul will be peaceful.

Teachers and their spiritual or religious movements are many here because your planet has the largest number of souls in your quadrant of the universe, and the teachers have all had recurring visits to this planet. Therefore, a soul may be more closely related to one belief or teaching depending upon prior exposure and soul growth with it. Past experience with certain teachers and their messages will then influence you toward the one spiritual group most able to bring you to enlightenment, or even a series of groups, as you rapidly move upward in this Time of Awakening's accelerating consciousness. But all of these groups are to combine now for the greater good and relinquish any tendency toward disunity.

As the gift of soul mastery is offered this lifetime, know that all the great teachers and masters involved with the Earth's history and its present dilemma are back in a helping role, although some chose to be more active than others and to assume certain responsibilities. This does not mean any is better or more valuable. It means they volunteered their efforts in specific ways and for stipulated times.

I seriously recommend that you visualize an intense beam of golden energy focused in this quadrant of space, on Earth, so that the entire planet basks in its glow. Although the gift of Jesus and his resurrection is historically recorded, do you realize he stayed nearby to amplify my ray essence for a 2,000 year plan to remind each sleeping soul's awareness of its prior

agreement as a caretaker of Earth? Thus you have been receiving increments of evolutionary support and energy from 22
percent at the resurrection time of Jesus up to 67 percent this
past November 17, 1986.

We are here to give the strength, the knowledge, and the
caring to get you over the last threshold into planetary enlightenment.

The energies we have given or filtered through to the Earth
for these 2,000 years allow progression of spiritual enlightenment.

Examine humanity's progress in the chart below for some
idea of present advancement rate. By examining this consciousness increase over the past 2,000 years, you will notice
the events that have occurred in the physical world as an
expression of our amplified energy and attention.

Enlightenment chart of spiritual evolution on Earth.

Percent	Event
100	Time of Radiance, yet to come
67	November 17th, 1986, evaluation by Higher Forces
62	Spring, 1986, Silver Ray energy focused for planetary concern
58	1938, spiritual knowledge available but not accepted by many
56	Background for Founding of USA
38	Magna Carta
22	33 AD or resurrection of Jesus
3	4 BC

Because of his persistent love and caring, a being formerly
called Jesus is the present coordinator of our activities and acts
as World Teacher designee. He has never failed to heal hu-

manity's emotional nature, grant forgiveness, and encourage the *positive* emotions you were created to express. His devoted willingness to remain with you to the end of this cycle speaks of a deep spiritual service few would give, but he is not to be deified. He is your example and model as he, himself, said. Christianity has misunderstood him as a savior. He, and millions of other energies, work together on the Gold Ray to cleanse and purify your soul during this critical hour. Let their example of unity be your own so the combined value and strength will not be lost.

In the higher dimensions where the Silver Ray uses a nine-member Supreme Council of Creation to assist in further creation, there is also a specialized creation of my own called Sananda who expresses my essence in the Omniverse. For this critical time Sananda particularly uses my Gold Ray in the 12th Universe, its galaxies, your solar system, and around Earth. This includes humanity but also what you call space brothers and sisters. Between the energies of Jesus and Sananda are other levels of responsibility, which do not need to be developed here. If you have contact with Krishna, Buddha, Mohammed, Moses, and other reknowned teachers, do not allow separation to occur in your response to them. All exist and all are necessary. Is this clear?

Sananda is my spokesperson and presently works to clarify and designate the relationship that you of Earth are to have with space beings and other lifeforms created by the Silver Ray. In the earlier epoch called Atlantis, your Earth related to these others with *karmic* implications that must now be resolved.

Then know this one's name, Sananda, because the times ahead may require galactic interchange, cooperation, and caring, based upon spiritual values.

As I leave you now to enjoy the true beauty of yourself and

your exquisite planet, please ponder what I have shared. Remember that God has *two energies*. COSMIC, the energized womb or endless connected fabric of space, and CREATIVE, the two specific energies born of God to bring forth many expressions of life and matter. These two *creative* energies are called the Gold and Silver Rays.

If you can begin to comprehend the context of *cosmic* and *creative* energy in their unique expressions, your relationship to God or First Cause will be enriched and your understanding of life expanded immeasurably.

Know that your soul is now officially called to learn and express peaceful measures, and set aside personality limitations of pride, anger, greed, fear, guilt, and separation. *There will only be* **three** *callings for each human to become peaceful, and no more*. This is officially your first unless you have information to the contrary.

Each soul is known about, cared about, has a life experience or identification number. Each soul is recorded in the knowledge of creation. It is because we care that you are given as many as three opportunities to fulfill your soul purpose. Yes, we understand the difficulty you have in differentiating energies called negative and positive, unholy or holy, dark or light. You may be confused and stumble for a while, even deny or reject. But in time you will grasp the great and positive caring that we of the light, or higher forces, have for you. Try to find within yourself the inspiration to accept and encourage others to hold onto hope. Know that all things and events for peace have been put in the realm of possibility, but you must support them.

In the name of our Parent, or First Cause, I now signify that you can be re-identified as a Caretaker of Planet C-ton if you have not already made such an agreement. If you choose to help complete the task of peace, you will be released from all prior spiritual misdeeds recorded during your 8-million-year soul journey here. You will be forgiven for everything actual or imagined in return for your soul pledge and practice to seek only peace and to care for the planet and all lifeforms throughout your lifetime. Take this unprecedented opportunity, dweller of Earth. You are truly needed to establish the stability of a *lasting* peace and restore the divine proclamation of your origin.

The Gold Ray
delivered by
Sananda, Lord of the Omniverse

Chapter III

The Great Rays

Before you can understand who you really are as a soul, you will need to comprehend both types of God-energy just explained—that which is *cosmic* and that which is *creative*. These concepts and principles may be new, but we ask you to listen carefully and ponder well. This knowledge is so vital that we shall say it frequently. Please remember!

Cosmic energy occurs in what you term space. Space is a vast interrelated web of God's energy, an apparent emptiness awaiting the birth of material life. This fertile expanse is so huge that to describe it takes the highest of your mathematics plus concepts you do not yet have. Suffice to say, it is a mammoth firmament awaiting the introduction of seeding or planting by *creative* energy to complete its fruitfulness.

It is vital for you to understand that space, not yet used or seeded, still contains all the ingredients or aspects of potential life. Thus, it is pregnant with opportunity for growth and creations of many kinds—gaseous material and solid objects from dust to galaxies. Therefore, please do not consider space empty. It is an atomic womb of sorts linked by God energy that allows creation to occur. When your unarmed technical devices leave the Earth, they do not all rent the fabric of space, but if they use any type of weaponry or force that is, itself, expressing energy for destructive purposes, damage is inevitable. The degree and type of damage varies, of course, depending upon the strength and caliber of the equipment. Then know these things, and do not let the invisible "fishnet" of creation be harmed by your devices, such as the proposed Star Wars weapons and others. Since this inexorable link of webbed energy holds other life forms and their material world in place, every serious rent must be repaired.

Know that this *cosmic* energy that God uses for birthing life is also a continuing flow necessary to support that which has already been created. Cosmic energy is the glue that holds created things together and relates them to each other. Its continual motion cradles and protects creation. The First Cause is the mighty source of this pregnant energy and even we, the Rays, do not know how it is made. But we perceive that it is ever-flowing without decrease or rest.

This cosmic energy oceans forth, ever replenishing, giving itself freely for the maintenance of all creation. This is why the universes and life can expand. Since we two Rays do not destroy our creations and the Great One continues to produce his cosmic energy, the universes expand unless life is destructive to itself or others. This is not to say there is no entropy, but entropy is a *natural* process compared to deliberate energy misuse and destructiveness.

Another kind of energy was needed to interact with the cosmic energy to create life at a physical level. This we term creative energy.

The compositions of these two energies are difficult to describe, but cosmic energy is similar to your idea of electromagnetic substance. Creative energy is more of a *force* of particles and molecules that can be intensified or softened when needed.

God's creative ability is described in your various world religions, but no one, *no one*, truly understands how God creates through the two Great Rays. To help you grasp what this *creative* energy actually is, ask yourself this question:

If cosmic energy is a fertile webbed fabric awaiting impregnation in that magnificent midnight blue expanse, then what would be needed to bring forth this implanting? How could things like gaseous substance and dense physical matter begin their interaction? Many scriptures have said that life was created by "the Word" or the wind of God's breath, will, or intention. However, that process has never been defined. The Word, or wind, that was thrust out by God had a second stage in which it was filled with creative energy. This creative energy of force or impulsion came about through decreased vibration—by twin powers—to avoid injuring the more delicate cosmic fabric.

As the Word, wind, or energy came forth, there was placed into unmanifested space an instantaneous birth of two immense energy streams which are called RAYS. These two rays came forth from God as two gigantic beams, colored gold and silver, each one-half mile wide and one mile long. We were still attached to our power source by what you on Earth would call an umbilical cord of energy. Thus we were birthed, yet retained connection to that which was our Parent. This act of reproduction completed a cycle intended by that Great One so it would have both a womb in which to place life and the needed process of using a different but balanced energy quality to fill it.

As the first two children of God, we Rays knew that we were to create, but in the beginning we did not know how. Does this seem strange? We were somewhat aware that we were light forces which could travel into space, but the details or clarity of that power were missing. Our Parent wished to remain in its own area and not move out into the far reaches of space; nonetheless, it wished for us and our creations to go forward limitlessly.

Measuring in your Earth time, it was probably a million years before we became mobile and began to experiment with our power. At first we just practiced extending and pulling back. Often we were playful as we learned about our capabilities, like infants exploring and learning from practice. We learned that we had the capability to generate from ourselves a beam of energy. This beam could be focused as a broad spectrum fanning out in any dimension or focused to a thin, very narrow pin-point. Its quality could be gentle or intensified. If you were to see the Rays, you would see sparkling silver light or a glowing golden light. These colors are on your planet in solidified form as your two precious metals. They have been put into your planet as a remembrance of God's offspring. Eventually we created many universes, lifeforms of all kinds, and worlds to boggle your imagination.

We create by putting particles or gaseous material together and then illuminating them. To you the process would seem magical, beyond belief. For us it is work with obvious responsibility, yet can be playful and joyous.

You should continue to think of God as the *ultimate* Creator, but it is his twin offspring who have created all physical matter and placed all life, even the life of souls, or energy beams, upon it. As true children of God, the Rays make those so-called heavenly bodies, like planets, stars, and the many physical expressions of solidity that eventuate into a galaxy or universe. In your 12th Universe, souls are energy rays or sparks brought into existence by the Silver Ray. I hasten to add that many of the matter-objects in space may not be the mere physical items that you perceive, but have spiritual quality and purpose.

We established your Sun, for example, which bursts with tremendous heat in explosive ways, to assure that your solar system would have physical energy for the growth and maintenance of all life. Yet many spirit energies reside there. It is a focal point to which your attention is drawn during the daytime hours. It turns your attention to space, the higher beings, or what you call God. In each human is an awareness of God, the First Cause.

The Sun is a creative item to balance and continue this circle of life upon the present nine planets, with two to come. It is also a reminder of the Gold Ray, but day is only one half of the full remembrance of God. The Silver Ray of moonlight and rainbows is the other half.

The power of the Gold or Silver Ray enables the human body to perceive colors. Within each color is a sound frequency. The creative energy of both Rays, then, is expressed as color and sound frequency.

The frequencies or vibrations are so high that your human senses cannot perceive them. Only in the rainbow's radiance do you glimpse a rare remembrance of light and color spectrum. In that moment you see reality and escape your planetary imprisonment. Nor can any Earth instrument record the high vibratory frequency of the Gold and Silver Ray energy, though X-rays, infra-red light, ultra-violet light, and gamma rays hint at a greater power.

Now, however, we want to raise your consciousness of our frequency, even though our vibration must be greatly lowered. In these coming days, humanity can tune into this lowered frequency and feel the vibration and intensity of these energies. These two vibrations are the closest experience for the human body and the Earth itself to know their creators on a frequency or sound basis.

Rarely, practically never, does God contact Earth. When our Parent does, it must be through a voice messenger or you would be destroyed. God's voice messenger was here August 1, 1985 with an 18 month ultimatum banning war and violence.

Because of humanity's adequate improvement during that 18 month period, the messenger returned on November 17, 1986, with a two-year extension of support for peace. We remind you again that *there is no direct communication with God.* It is a gross misunderstanding when people say that they talked to God! Even the Great Rays dare not linger in the Great One's presence.

Although you cannot directly contact God, still you have had the Gold Ray's energy around this planet for some 7 million years and the Gold Ray qualities are more than ultra-violet and solar energies. They go into the interwoven galaxies and universes of the Omniverse as ONE light. However, as explained, on your planet the Gold Ray expresses on a lowered frequency as the Christ Light or Christ Consciousness whereby souls can unify into one mind. The Silver Ray, on the other hand, allows humans to turn to self-sovereignty and is represented by subconscious healing. Like lunar, or feminine, energy the Silver Ray helps transform emotions into their higher vibrations.

A simple way to describe the Christ Consciousness of the Gold Ray is that it is like a flashlight. When you push the switch that beam of light equates with the Gold Ray's energy beam. His power is very great, but you cannot even imagine the distance it must travel. When it reaches your planet it broadens out to bathe the planet in a sustained beam of Christ Consciousness energy. Now, during this Time of Awakening, the Silver Ray is also amplifying the energy you receive through the moonlight and rainbow energies. However, neither the Christ energy nor the Silver Ray's seven-color spectrum beam of the rainbow are at their full force on Earth yet. Our amplification increased on November 17, 1986, though, so perhaps you have noticed something different since then? The difference is in the lighter vibration we beam upon you, which creates the impression that time has sped up! In fact, your experience of time will be increased nearly 20 percent by mid-November, 1987.

Yes, we are the creators of the many mansions; we are directly using God's energy, though our umbilical cords are more like a homing device now. With our Parent's support we bring your soul and all physical life into safety and sustain it there! Life is to be respected and preserved. Grasp that and you understand God and the Rays.

Now, are there questions you would ask?

QUESTIONS BY VIRGINIA ESSENE TO SILVER RAY
(Ann Valentin entranced)

V.   How does the Time of Awakening actually affect us on Earth?

S.R.   This Time of Awakening is a designated period during which the higher ray energies are being brought and focused as light or vibrations.   For those with spiritual awareness, an explanation about the rays will feel true.   You are to be aware that the seven colors of the rainbow energies are now amplified around your *entire* planet.   Have you not noticed a difference?

V.   How do they arrive here?

S.R.   Let me see if I can explain this to you.   Not only do we have what we call an envelope of the rainbow energies around the entire planet, but also the intensity of the Christ Consciousness is accentuated.   This gift has been amplified since November 17, 1986, so people will feel the energies of our great rays and the force of the purpose of each ray, matching those in their own soul.   This is a "soul calling" on our part. We want you to wake up.

V.   How did that color envelope get there?

S.R.   I put it there myself along with the energies that

worked with me earlier this year. Therefore, all souls will respond to the colors of their rays with more intensity than ever
before. For instance, people who have a blue ray as their main
ray of intention will be drawn to use their scientific and
technical data more than ever before *to improve the living
conditions on the planet, to preserve humanity.* Scientific
understanding should not in any way be used for
destructiveness, but each soul has free will, free choice of
actions.

V.   Have the Great Rays ever been here together on the
planet before?

S.R.   No, we have *never* been here all together like we are
now.

V.   Are you saying that in the whole 8 million years that
humanity has had a soul experience on the planet, that the Gold
and Silver Rays have never been here simultaneously?

S.R.   Yes, this would be the first time. But the danger you
create requires it. Even the seven great subrays or individual
color rays created by me are here. They have all been brought
together and intensified from the Silver Ray energy to establish
peace upon this planet.

V.   Silver Ray, you said you had to learn to create.
Could you explain that further?

S.R.   Let me see how to tell you about creation. We are
superintelligent *be*-ings or entities or forces; use the word
forces. We are superintelligent forces. We have the freedom
to do whatever we choose, whatever we think we can do. In
the first universes the Gold and Silver Rays worked together.
Rather than oppose each other or have conflict, we later
specialized or chose different emphases, but we are united even
in our differences.

To balance these energies the Gold Ray decided to be the
force that you call will and power. The Silver Ray energy be-

came totally creative and then eventually nurtured these creations. But this was not done in the very beginning. If I have to give you some sort of timeframe, this might have been equivalent to a trillion years after we were created, but that is only a guess, for it is so far in antiquity that I cannot pin-point time on it.

V.   A question that is always asked is ... who made God?

S.R.   Even I do not know that. God was there.

V.   Has he ever explained this to you? Have you ever asked him?

S.R.   No. There is no beginning; the energy was just there.

V.   My finite mind cannot grasp that. It seems that something had to cause it. What was the cause of God?

S.R.   There is no way of knowing that. God has always been, and has always been this powerful, so far as we know.

V.   Is there a force or a power beyond God that would indicate God is not the very first Creator?

S.R.   I follow your question, but let us just say that God, the First Cause, is all in all. It is beyond pure white light. It is crystal.

V.   Did this great being, God, ever tell you why he decided to create things of himself?

S.R.   God did not want to move its own energy to another location. God did not want to utilize its powers in any *direct* way, but it desired creation to manifest physically. This combined cosmic and creative energy was the solution. Obviously, this book could change many concepts about creation and God. God is the original source for everything, but it does not do everything personally, as your Earth religions tend to suppose.

V.   What was it like, suddenly realizing that you were born and had all these powers?

S.R.   The word surprise is a good word because we had to

decide what we were to do, now that we had been created. We could communicate with each other, so we discussed our purpose.

V.   At that time did God communicate with you?

S.R.   It was as if the God force were watching us, silently, and at the same time monitoring us to see what we were going to do, what our intelligence was, and how we were going to use it.

V.   Did you ever have the feeling that the Creator did not know exactly how it was going to turn out when he created you?

S.R.   I cannot answer that. We were never told not to do a certain thing. We were never questioned in our creativity.

V.   Then you were never given an "instruction book" on how to do all this?

S.R.   No.

V.   Ideas? Suggestions? Directions?

S.R.   No. We were there for some time and did not do anything; we just were. Then we experimented, discovered our capabilities, and discussed the results.

V.   Did you intermingle your energies to discuss this?

S.R.   No, we did not intermingle energies. We were aware that we were separate. We would come close and would vibrate, but we never mingled the energies.

V.   What did you think would happen if you did?

S.R.   An entanglement that would prevent separating again. We understood that we were to be separate.

V.   How did you know that you had powers you were supposed to use?

S.R.   This became a knowingness within each of us, an energizing to move forward. We received impulses to move.

V.   You mean in a physical way you moved through space?

S.R.   *Into* space.   At first there was nothing, so it was moving forward *into* space.

V.   And how did you know what to do then?

S.R.   I believe, as I tell you, that it came through the impulses of the God force energy.   The cosmic space was receptive to everything we did.   Nothing was rejected.   It was as if the space itself was waiting for matter to be created within it.

V.   So it always felt welcoming?

S.R.   Yes.   It was very receptive.   The first item that we created was a very, very small planet.   If you were to view it, it would look like a large round ball.

V.   When you say "we," did you work together with the Gold Ray on that?

S.R.   Yes.   We worked together for eons of time.

V.   Just making that first little perfect universe?

S.R.   Yes.   Then we learned to make that which you call stars, other lifeforms, some moons.   The universes are full of life only because we were creative.   We have much creative energy, and in the beginning it was very, very strong, perhaps excessively so, as you might view it now.   But we came on with great energizing.   We kept creating, creating, and creating.   Now, by comparison, our creativity is subdued, and much of our efforts are spent just watching or taking care of that which has been created.

V.   Are you saying you have not made anything lately?

S.R.   Not to the degree that we did in the past.   There is no end to the universe.   There is no end to space.   And I hope you will understand that this will always be, since the God force is continually vibrating cosmic energy.

Of course much of this God force energy is absorbed into that which has already been created, and it definitely continues to energize all of the areas that you call space.   But there is far more cosmic energy than can be absorbed and used by the existing creations. This is why your scientists are aware that space is unlimited. It just goes on and on in nearly every direction.

V.   We had a question from a man in England saying that it seemed to him twelve was a very small number of universes, and he felt it was not correct.

S.R.   There are more creations, yes, but they are not developed into universes.

V.   Can you describe the first ray you created (now called the Rebel Ray)?

S.R.   It is very beautiful with all colors entwined. This is why it has been able to create the illusion of godliness and deter people away from our parent Creator. It is not dark and ugly as the biblical Satan or fallen angel is sometimes described. Can you accept this?

V.   This is one question frequently asked of us. Who or what is God and what does s/he look like?

S.R.   Many have asked what God looks like and, since we two Rays are the only ones who can enter into the inner ring without harm, I shall describe it for you. We are also providing a sketch you can now examine.

In size I could compare it to something in your solar system like the Earth's Moon. God's energy circumference is perhaps four times larger than your Moon and is filled with the most intense white light energy you can imagine. It is rather circular or roundish in form and has at its very core a center about the size of a ten story building.

This elongated, somewhat cylindrical core is beyond description in its force. Even we would be destroyed if we ventured too close. This core of intense crystal light has intelligence and monitors back to itself, through us, all the information of the various universes. You might describe it as the all-knowing channel. When information goes through us, it is instantly absorbed and understood. Your technical people would understand this as a caring self-created memory bank of unbelievable proportion and infinite computational ability.

This God force energy is both the beginning and the ending of a loop that feeds through us its own intention and messages. Thus, it is fed by the many levels from the first dimension of reality right on up through your third dimension and our 22nd level. The many universes' information goes upward through the various rays I created and is filtered back to God after its last stop with the Rays. God's multi-levels are inexpressible. God truly is all-knowing, cosmically cognizant, omnipresent, omnipotent, and omniscient.

God is absolutely awesome. Yet, it has a caring aspect, also. God is not a machine. God is a Creator who retains interest and concern in the affairs of the many worlds, dimensions, and realities that we Rays, the outpoured energies of God's light, have created in cosmic space.

If you can grasp that this unspeakable One is the giver of cosmic and creative energy, and that all life would die without it, you will realize each human should truly revere and respect this One. You may be physically far from its immediate environment, but God has noted and acted on the dilemma of Earth's present situation.

By that Great One's intervention, you are a quarantined planet until peace is established and your hydrogen explosions and nuclear weaponry cease forever.

By this description of God you must surely realize no Earth dweller has ever spoken directly to God. A few may have had messages carried through the angelic or high spiritual realms, but prayers to God are normally handled by your individual teachers, guides, and guardian angels. As mentioned, only on the rarest of occasions does this Mighty One send a voice messenger to Earth to relay information, proclamations, or guidance. One such rare directive by God on August 1, 1985, demanded peace. This event clarified our own plans. Truly, you are under the scrutiny of the Creator, at this time, as well as our own. It was that One who required you to begin a new path to peace, and it is because of that request, primarily, that we shower you with our attention and assistance.

These additional two years of support will probably end in December of 1988, unless there are unforeseen changes. It is partly why I have come to energize your own soul rays. But we will keep you informed of changes as they occur.

It is with serious intent that I make this last statement. God has warned you to cease your underground hydrogen explosions and atomic and nuclear *weaponry*. These energies are not to be negatively utilized at any time for any reason. I trust that this statement is absolutely clear. Time is truly critical. We support your actions to make these necessary changes at once.

Let your heart sing a melody called "save all life, bring peace to Earth," and as others join you a mighty chorus of intention shall jointly create a new harmony.

It shall be a new harmony for life this time, have no doubt. And we shall add our own music to celebrate with your pure vibration. Then where time ends, we shall meet at the completion of your tear-stained journey in recognition of a job well done.

So be it then.

Chapter IV

Your Soul's Origin and Purpose

Perhaps you have wondered who you really are and why you find yourself living on this particular planet called Earth? Nearly everyone asks "Who am I? Why was I born? What is life all about?"

Religious and spiritual teachings tell you that you are a soul, not a mere physical body. But what is a soul, and how do you experience it? How can you contact this remote, intangible thing?

Our only purpose is to help you answer these questions not just intellectually but at an experience level. Through the words and the illustrations in this book, we intend that you finally realize the truth, for the remembrance is within you. We wish you to begin experiencing your soul connection and using its guidance for your life decisions.

Because you have chosen to read this material, you are well on your way to more inner soul knowing, for our words will trigger your recollection. You are a soul. Never doubt this. But what is a soul? Is it some fleeting dream, some improbable imagining? No, your soul is the only lasting part of you, and it has actual physical properties which reside within the body.

The soul is a narrow beam of energy created by God's first two children, the Gold and Silver Rays. It is condensed and amplified with a spark of life, the element of movement that responds to the frequencies of cosmic energy. Because the God force is energy, the Great Rays are energy. As these Great Rays willingly created things for God, souls were made of that same ingredient, energy. The correct understanding of the expression, "you are made in God's image and likeness," would be that your soul is energy, but in much smaller measure than God's or the Great Rays'.

Most spiritual teachings on Earth have not clearly defined what a soul is, leaving the issue of soul identity to confusion or disbelief. But then, only recently has your technological understanding increased to allow this realization. There are, and have been, those so-called "mystery schools" that have preserved much knowledge about such things, but it is necessary now for *all of humanity* to know and use the knowledge, lest your negative attitudes and acts of violence continue unabated. You must realize that the small membership of an elite group of knowers has not made an appreciable difference in Earth's behavior as a planet, and this must change immediately!

Each soul is to awaken now and express goodness through its human personality for the welfare of all concerned. What is the Time of Awakening? It is the time for *soul awareness* and application of spiritual respect and dedication to God, but it is also a time of caring for your planet and all life upon it. For you see, dear ones, if you do this one task which you agreed to do some 8 million years ago, your soul will be returned to its former glory, and you will be able to advance in the great spiritual mansions, dominions, or planes of existence.

Yes, you came to Earth as one of its first caretakers or were created later as a child of those early ones. In either case, you are vital to our present plan. Perhaps, as I tell the story of the soul and its visit to Earth, you will remember or at least sense

46

the truth.

I have said you are a soul or a created physical substance called energy. What does this mean? The soul is a brilliant golden white creation of light energy *without a physical body*. Eons ago it was a flat vertical beam about seven feet from top to bottom. You were truly a spark—or small ray like God—made by one of those two first-born creations of God, the Great Rays.

In this 12th Universe the Silver Ray's energy pulsed you into a molecular flash of light and life, as a separate identity from all the other "soul sparks." So you had no physical body when you were first divinely impulsed. You were a *glowing brilliance* from a higher vibratory residence who lived in a spiritual dimension far beyond that of Earth. Even now you are particles of light—cosmic energy! Is this hard to believe? Then picture a flash of lightning or electricity as your model. For though you now reside within a physical body, the soul identity remains within, scaled down after 7 million years of cramped physical encasement. That soul anxiously awaits its final release and graduation as an accredited caretaker of Earth. Is it unbelievable that you have shrunk in soul size and we have been trying to bring you back to that former radiance? Unbelievable that in this Time of Awakening we are here to assure this transition will occur for those who seek it?

Then let me tell you a story about how it happened and allow you to ponder its meaning for yourself. For we were there. We know. Now it is appropriate for you to remember, as well.

You have already learned that the Great Rays are capable of creating anything they wish whether it be physical objects, such as gases and matter for planets and stars, or various lifeform types, including the soul. Trillions or more of these beams of energy had already been created in your 12th Universe, and many were living in locations around the Milky

Way galaxy. Thus, there were already many bodyless souls, seven foot high, in existence.

When the Silver Ray and the Supreme Council of Creation deemed that their most beautiful creation in the universe was ready for development, a recruitment program was undertaken to select about one million scientific caretakers to be the work team upon C-ton.

The great director of the Blue Ray, Archangel Michael, was in charge of this recruitment process, and many from existing planets were asked if they would like to apply for this assignment. Because the planet was so unique and beautiful in its exquisite varieties of the plant, mineral, and animal kingdom creations, and the volunteers would have a rare opportunity to assist in the development of additional botanical and biological forms, many souls wished to go. A "small" soul, so to speak, is rarely given the opportunity to be a co-creator, to monitor the development of lifeforms and help them adapt. Each prospective caretaker was interviewed, in your terms, and eventually the group was organized for this expedition into one of the farthest reaches of the known universe.

Please remember that each soul agreed to complete a contract of caring for the planet and honoring God until the entire mission was finished, even as today you may sign up for a certain period of employment or until a project is done. Because the planet was to be a free will planet, each soul would have to agree to assist in the development of millions of new life types and to stay until the job was done. It was the most novel experiment in the 12th Universe! But it has never been finished, as your present experience on Earth indicates.

Can you imagine the mammoth excitement and feeling of adventure those who made the agreement to go might have had?

Now you might like to know that nearly 80 percent of that

first million souls were selected from two major sites—what you call the Pleiades cluster and the constellation of Orion. Why these places? Because their stable societies valued justice and respected God, and the souls living in these areas personified these values in their cultures. Some volunteers were accepted from other stars such as Sirius and nearby constellations, and many among you call these aforementioned areas "home." There were only a few from another universe who volunteered.

If you can grasp and accept that these souls came of their own free will to work in developing millions of new species to further beautify the planet C-ton, you will understand the setting of our story. Please pause here a moment to see how you feel about what is being shared.

Remember that none of these souls who came together in that original armada of free will beings had ever lived in anything but a high spiritual vibration of cooperation and caring. Thus, it was a comparatively easy task for the entire group to live harmoniously and attend to the details of the planet's needs—to the further development of various botanical and biological lifeforms—without excessive direction. They were quite capable of harmonious existence and service. Although Archangel Michael was the coordinator, he was frequently absent after the initial stage of the work had been accomplished to the satisfaction of all concerned.

These soul energies were nearly identical in form due to their high spiritual level and were not so separate, or individualized, as you "fallen ones" of Earth are today. It may be difficult to imagine how a beam of energy could "work" without arms and legs and a torso like yours, but recall that they are very intelligent with the power to move objects mentally, not physically. They could also monitor the lifeforms by electrical impulses that were then stored in something like a data bank.

You may visualize this collection and storage area as near the top of the energy beam.

Each soul began to acquire memory of its own experiences, because each soul had separate tasks to accomplish. One soul energy worked with a particular type of tree, rock, seaform, plant, or flower. Another worked with water, air, and so on. No two had *identical* experiences on the dense physical planet to which they had immigrated.

The uniqueness of each soul, then, has been acquired from its intelligence, its recorded experience called memory, and free will. As each soul became deeply concerned about the lifeforms under its care, its own soul uniqueness was increasingly modified. Thus it could and did adapt through the great experience of variety so unusual on C-ton.

Nonetheless, since there was great activity and satisfaction with the work, and all souls were of the pure and holy light, this adventure continued for—in your time frame—about 800,000 years. Life was stable, caring, communally organized, and filled with loyal relationships. For those who had come it seemed no time at all because they maintained the oneness of life, using God's cosmic energy from the north, to keep them in attunement. Also, due to the amount of important tasks, an additional volunteer contingency of 10 million souls arrived about 200,000 years after the original emigration. Joyously there were now many more helpers to assist! And timelessly they continued the great experiment.

This unity and joyousness came into a serious challenge, however, with the event referred to in your holy books as the "separation." This part of the story is extremely sad but must be related for you to grasp what is happening now.

Do you recall there was that minor ray—the Rebel Ray—that had been created by the Silver Ray but had left his parent's area? The Rebel Ray now decided to try to win the reverence of these C-ton souls and to take over the planet's beauty as a base for his own power. So he came as the age-old deceiver, surreptitiously, with wily ways rather than force. Like a despicable charmer, he began his evil intention to claim Earth for his own purposes.

Now, you must remember, these souls had never experienced evil. Never. And they were not expecting an enemy, so there was no call for assistance to the home forces of light. Almost before they knew what had occurred, some souls were beguiled by the Rebel Ray who used intelligence at first, and later on what is called sound frequency, to distort their reverence for God and concern for their work. His persuasion and sound-frequency influence confused some soul creations.

How did this affect the souls, you may ask? This outside influence caused the physical quality of their light to diminish because they began to turn away from the northern direction of God's inflowing energy. They faced the south and lost contact with God. This is what is meant by turning away from the light. Over time these souls grew dimmer because they were no longer being recharged by the God force.

As long as they had looked to God with belief, recognition, and remembrance, they were safe. It is truly a lesson sadly learned that the Rebel Ray turned them away from God, for his vibrations and frequency were not pure, and the souls lost their high spiritual glow. It was now impossible for them to return home.

Only at this late hour did the Blue Ray of Michael learn of the situation, yet he immediately went to the defense of the holy light workers. Again, it is with great sadness we report that he was unable to defeat the Rebel Ray and, without reinforcements, heaven lost its intense fearsome battle.

By the time reports came into the heavenly realms and help could have been dispatched, it was too late. And so began the

51

great creative challenge to the God force through the Gold and Silver Rays! How could they save those endangered souls?

This tale has been told in many ways upon your planet in the various religious teachings, yet few truly know what happened next and why. Let this now be common knowledge upon your planet and in the hearts of humanity.

The Gold Ray immediately directed his energy through the 12th Universe, especially around Earth, to amplify God's energy for the souls still able and willing to receive it. The energy of that act, 7 million years ago, has been maintained ever since, so that your soul group would not be left comfortless. This Gold Ray energy is what you now call the Christ Light or the Christ Consciousness. Finally, the Silver Ray acted also, and assigned each soul an invisible guardian to help and care for it.

Because cosmic agreements must always be honored, it was still necessary for the diminishing souls to complete their planetary caretaking functions and achieve the mastery that went with that promise. Souls would have to be brought back to their original level of course, but they needed to be retained on the Earth, also, to finish their chosen task. Thus, the Silver Ray's plan of soul completion is culminating on your Earth during this Time of Awakening.

By the Time of Radiance the deserving souls will be raised back to their higher spiritual essence, and they will also have the satisfaction of saving Earth from its possible demise, for negativity and war are still humanity's trademark.

With great skill and willingness the Silver Ray planned a physical container in which to hold the fading, dimming soul rays until they could be raised back to a higher dimension. The container would be known to you, today, as a physical body, a temple for the soul to use during its experiences on the planet. The body was created as self-healing and capable of living forever. It was the eternal fountain of youth your books speak about. Then, a thousand years was nothing unusual for a lifetime. Does it not seem miraculous for a cut to heal or a bone to mend itself? Your soul was thereby given a great gift.

It was expected that all souls would choose to return to the God force and release personal desire for power and control over others. But you see, that has still not occurred, so the higher forces are here with one last offer of restitution.

If you could see all of the many body packages prepared in the various universes, you would appreciate the particular design of your own physical container. It is truly one of the finest examples of form. It is almost an ultimate design, so practical and useful is its pattern.

We call this body a "soul container." It is a functional machine that enables the soul to accomplish its purposes on the physical plane.

The brain is a storage unit that works through the intelligence of the soul, which relates to the mind. The brain sends impulses down through the body to allow motion or responses to its exterior and interior experiences. The five senses, as you call them, allow this body machine to operate smoothly, making instantaneous adjustments at such a high frequency that you are not even aware of their occurrence. This design allows the body to protect itself, continue its life, and adapt itself to the environment or change the environment where needed.

We want you to understand the relationship of the human body to the soul, to the Earth, and to all of creation. The body is connected to the Earth because it is made of the Earth's elements! It allows the soul to be here for a designated time period, in your sequence of events, for completion of the planetary experiment.

Now, the planetary experiment is primarily what you call free will. As you begin to understand these things, you remove the element of mystery, and it becomes factual. Although there have been difficulties for the souls during this adventure, the experiment has not been a failure because each soul, regardless of what is happening to it, even under adverse circumstances, still wants to be attuned to the God force. Hence, you have spiritual feelings or religious attitudes. The focus of each soul has been recognition of, and reverence for, the God force. Existence is very simple; it is being aware for a purpose.

But personalities have added an element of glamour or mystery to their awareness by false perception. Repetitive incarnations are partly responsible for adding layers over the soul's purity. Obviously, if you have layers of past negative behavior to relieve, you are not existing in the same way, because then you are on a pattern that *requires* certain activities. You are no longer totally free in your beingness. We now release souls from this past negativity, if they wish peace and will be truly reborn back into pure intention as caretakers of the Earth.

Now, if you can grasp that you are energy and your body design lives through vibrations and frequencies, which you are always giving off, you can use your mind to control these vibrations. The field of energy around the outside of the body is called the aura. Your aliveness, or aura, is one large field of energy, then, constantly responding to your environment; it is the totality of all the life events you have experienced. It is the grandiose sum of everything you have done and learned, but it is different than the rays that we will discuss later.

When the "separated" caretakers were offered a refuge for their diminishing light, souls responded differently to the offer and to the experience of a body. Some eventually raised themselves back to a higher vibrational quality, and some did not.

Souls that became "contained" could still come and go during sleep, and some went farther and longer than others.

But over a period of time, they became more and more sealed in their bodies, and the soul within shrunk to the four to six inches high that you have within you today. This accelerated soul shrinking is sometimes referred to in your literature as the "fall," not to be confused with the "separation," when souls turned away from the cosmic energy of God.

We call this period the "time of fear's great influence." You see, before the great battle, fear had *never* been experienced by the souls. But when fear registered as an experience for the first time, the soul pulled in, which caused shrinking. The intelligence stayed intact, but now there was a negative emotional response for the first time. The souls were further confused and distorted by fear.

Most of those souls have never fully recovered, for as the separation occurred within each human being, he or she became distrustful. The love factor was no longer evident; humans began to change. They now had to prove themselves to each other. As a result, suspicion was rampant.

This poignant separation from security to fear took some thousands of years, even though the battle itself, between the Rebel Ray and Michael, was very quick. Then, in the body, Earth life changed dramatically, as the separated relationship of soul to soul, being to being, occurred. It became similar to what you have now. Great civilizations have come and gone, but the basics of your physical existence have not changed much. When you "modern" people read ancient historical accounts, you are amazed at the similarity in human behavior. This is because of "the fall."

The threefold rescue plan previously described—Gold Ray's beam of support, Silver Ray's assignment of a guardian angel, and the body container's creation—moved very slowly. The souls could leave their physical bodies for brief sojourns to assist in soul recollection of God, and they had assigned guardian forces for comfort. But they forgot, nonetheless. Even the Christ Consciousness which beamed down courage, comfort, and strength had no major effect.

We were certain the ultimate goal of returning to the original purpose was possible, but it seemed as if it would take eons of time upon your plane where suffering is prevalent. Therefore, we have always endeavored to guide the souls incarnated here so that they would never feel alone or abandoned. But our project to return your soul to its former power and beauty has languished, causing much human pain.

To bring this into balance now, and allow freedom of choice to each soul, we currently institute the great plan of restitution. At last, if you wish, you can choose once again to be an Earth caretaker—and thereafter either return to your home place, or remain here on Earth for the Time of Radiance—experiencing joy and beauty!

We cannot presently change the size of your small soul, but we are helping you increase the size of its wattage. With the knowingness and acceptance of the God force as a full power energizing life and existence on your planet, with meditation and service to humanity, the personal soul light within you starts to increase. So, even though you are a soul within your body container, your radiance extends beyond your human body. The power of a flashlight is not contained within the flashlight itself, but in the batteries. Your soul is your battery, and as your wattage increases, your illumination increases. Then you are actually perceived more brightly!

Meanwhile, you are earthbound except for your out-of-body excursions, when the soul uses an intensely compacted energy "homing device," or sensor of electrical impulses called "silver cord," which is attached to a spiritual home base elsewhere. Be assured in the Time of Radiance your soul size will increase. You are regaining some light amplification now. This is possible primarily because the Silver Ray has given a "ray of intention" for each soul. This will be explained more fully in another chapter.

Part of the ultimate plan is that, upon review of soul experiences, there will be energizing, rejuvenating, and recharging for the souls who wish to return to their home planet after an adjustment period.

Now we must explain one final aspect about what your soul does between its earthly visitations. Many of you have been taught, refreshed, and assisted in the higher realms, not only during sleep and meditation, but also after that transition from physical incarnation. These higher realms are your genuine spiritual habitat, so listen within as we clarify.

We explain this so you will not fear death if it should come before the Time of Radiance. Prepare yourself to go to the highest spiritual level *now* by correct earthly behavior. Do not put it off. Become peace-loving at once. Use your influence to help heal the planet. Reject all thoughts of planetary war. Make a difference!

Now what are these higher spiritual levels, you may wonder, since you on Earth are on level 3.6.

Level four of the higher realms is for the souls who are still attached very closely to Earth by their thoughts and desires. Because they are still attracted to their Earth experiences, they are not able to go a step beyond to purer soul perception. Some souls may leave their physical body, then, but they have not left the energy area of the physical planet itself. Level four is certainly a higher level than three, where you are now, but it is not the level that the soul truly wishes for spiritual progression. From level four it is easy to return into the Earth plane with its many desires and limitations. It is a stepping stone, but not a high one.

Now, the fifth level is much higher than the fourth level,

and it is one where the soul can have truer perception of its existences, whether they be long past, just past, or the accumulation of many lives.

Level six is almost an in-between stage. Energies who make a transition there are not fully ready to return, but they are not fully cleansed, either. In other words, the intent of the soul's schooling is not completed yet.

The seventh level is higher still, for here a soul has purity of intention, but it continues to work toward level ten where mastery is truly achieved.

There are but a few souls on levels eight and nine, although some high teachers reside there. As you have advanced educational degrees on Earth, these souls are also preparing for their higher step to ten.

Level ten responsibilities and activities extend beyond your own planet. Some souls might still relate to Earth, but not as specifically as from nine down. Tasks could involve solar or galactic record keeping or intercommunications extending out to the universe itself. Beyond your solar system are many higher levels of service you will learn about in due time.

Some of your space brothers and sisters are on spiritual levels four, five, and a few on six. So do not think them Gods!

But back to Earth's spiritual level 3.6, all souls here—even the nearly 5 billion offspring of the fallen ones—are eligible for spiritual movement to these higher levels. By choosing to take care of the physical planet, you can be freed. In the past, the soul was required to come back into another bodyframe until it had fulfilled the terms of the soul contract that it had made, but reincarnation can now be set aside for those loving souls who express their highest caring behavior to the planet and all of life. This is a magnificent gift to be treasured!

Take the greatest advance for your soul that you can, then. Also, help your many spiritual soul mates do the same. Help because you know it is the right thing. Take no shortcuts, and leave no kind thought or deed unexpressed.

Each soul is called to participate in this final chapter of awakening. None are excused or omitted. Hasten to your calling with devotion and caring, and let your attitude and behavior accrue their notice where all is known and recorded. All souls must demonstrate their mettle, their commitment, and their caring. It is your long awaited hour, souls of the Great Rays. Let your actions on the cosmic camera be memorable.

Let us sing together our ancient melody as these final days are wisely used. Then, in the shimmering beauty of half-remembered yesterdays, may the light in your soul burst forth like the blossoming of a radiant spring bouquet, intent on glory's name.

Welcome, caretaker of the Earth, into the remembrance of your true reality where the One spiritual family is forevermore your identity and membership.

Chapter V

Your Ray of Intention:
A Cosmic "Soul Print"

Did you know you have a cosmic "soul print" of spectacular color? Yes, your soul has brought an unusual gift along with it for this lifetime, during the period called Time of Awakening. It is an inner guidance system called *rays*. These brilliantly colored rays describe your soul's purpose and intention, even if you and other humans can't see them yet. This "ray of intention" helps you accomplish your soul motives, interests, and actions. It is your cosmic "soul print" to those of us who perceive your colors. We know exactly why you are here. Have you ever wondered why you have been interested in the things you like? Or what it is that makes "you" you? For there is no one else identical anywhere on Earth!

Many people find these "why do I behave the way I do?" questions embarrassing because they seldom or never stop to ponder such things. Perhaps you have. But whether you think you know yourself or not, the good news is that, even if you cannot *see* your rays you can *hear* the true soul of you sending messages from inside. Therefore, you must be still and listen lest you miss the whole point of your current life on the planet! Kindly consider that your soul has a special beam of energy with colored rays contained in your physical body, and let us now explain how the rays carry your life purpose in their various colors. This group of colored energy beams constitutes your cosmic calling card or "soul print."

Now please pause and look at the colored illustration on "the soul's ray of intention" before we proceed.

As we keep repeating, the Time of Awakening is a special time upon your planet. Each soul, having had previous incarnations, selects a main purpose to complete this final self-mastery cycle. This soul purpose is amplified and carried life-long through one colored ray with one or more supplemental rays next to it. Each ray is energized with purpose and vibration. This ray constellation may have anywhere from two to seven color bands of varying widths, but the first color is the largest band and bears your major life intention. Everything you need to know about your soul's choice or reason for coming to Earth is stated in this simple, direct way to keep you on course.

Within your chest cavity area (for most adults), you are a soul-blaze of brilliant light streaming up and down through the center of your body. This light carries stabilizing messages stating why you came here, what you intended to accomplish, and the interests and activities that would most greatly benefit your primary soul purpose. This ray group radiates down into the Earth's gravitational pull to attach you to the Earth and shimmers three feet over your head to receive the spiritual vibrations we send you during the Time of Awakening.

Now you may ask how it is possible to have this wondrous "soul print."

Your rays come with the soul into the baby's body and begin like a thin, almost invisible energy thread. This thread is activated when the human infant is born, and it starts to grow and expand. As the child grows physically, the rays "unwind" and mature within the being. By age 14 the main ray of intention then extends three feet above the head so it can relate to our incoming invisible energies outside the body. Your tightly compacted ray radiances reach full maturity at approximately 28 years of age and are glorious to see. When I or any of the Lords of Light view your body, it is the primary way you are identified to us. Here is the truth of you boldly, colorfully displayed.

The size of the soul at birth is generally from four to six inches high. This is why children are usually born 16 to 20-odd inches in length. They must sustain the balance of this soul energy. I have frequently told you that the body is a container! Do not be insulted by this. At "the fall," when your soul quality had "shrunk" and your light was getting dark, we had to put it in something until we could help it regain its former intensity and vibration. If I may jest, you have been living in "soul storage" for about 6 million years. However, this is the very first time we have given you these soul rays with our special addition of cosmic wisdom and spiritual discernment included within them.

Remember that when souls were placed in physical bodies, death began, and so reincarnation became a temporary necessity until souls could complete their original contracts as caretakers of the Earth. In those times beings just came back into the body with the soul inside. They had other spiritual beings guiding them, of course, but there were no *inner rays*. At first, they still had a keen awareness of the Earth and the universe, but with each incarnation the memory of the God force grew dimmer.

What you call worship or the religious aspect of life became further removed. There have been some highly evolved spiritual civilizations; however, the majority of people fell away from this great knowing. Now we bring you a time of enlightenment where the focus is changing back to God-reverence or appreciation. We instituted the gift of the ray of intention to change humanity's behavior quickly. This light we now focus to stimulate your rays is your passport home.

The rays inside of you were originally created in this universe and on this planet by the Silver Ray, the matrix or container of all seven colors known to you on Earth. In this way, the Silver Ray is the maker of your rainbow and has brought the entire seven color spectrum into visibility for the human eye to see and joyously remember. There is *no* other planet on which these seven colors can be observed simultaneously as you have them here. This rainbow, or arc of beautiful color, excites most humans who witness it. The invisible is made visible for a moment, and your soul rejoices at seeing *reality*. For your personality lives in an illusion where you are spiritually blind. Actually, colors are ever present behind the veil of your lost consciousness, and one day you will see them again all around you!

When your soul looks out through the eye windows and sees the rainbow, it remembers reality and your own origin as God's energy. No wonder you respond to rainbows. This is what you are: energy, light, color. You are a dancing cosmic vibration.

Part of the basic design built into the human body machine, then, is *the ability for you to observe colors and relate to them*. When in balance this ability harmonizes your negative and positive emotions so that they are kept on an even keel. A balanced use of all seven colors can bring peaceful emotions, but if a color is missing or impure, negative emotions result. You are a ray, which actually vibrates to color and sound frequencies. Your eyes *see* color and your skin *feels* color.

In New Teachings for an Awakening Humanity the vibrant cosmic energy colors in the book's cover announced that the essence of life on Earth is color. Perhaps it was an *un*conscious response, but response there was. The Time of Awakening is the activating and amplifying of each soul's ray of intention; it is a call to action for peace.

Your holy books have statements that a "bow" would be put in the sky as a reminder of God's covenant. But how many think of this? Yet even the so-called irreligious can appreciate the rainbow and its colored splendor that carries a message beyond words. Its radiance is a sign from the past and a promise for both present and future. Rainbows are full of wonder, for they open your remembrance to, and experience of, color and sound. They are gifts from our invisible realm.

The energies of the rainbow are very powerful, and it is hoped that the Earth will finally know the glory of these energies, especially during this Time of Awakening. You will need them during the Time of Reckoning, and in the Time of Radiance you will know the full potential of these rays and their energy.

Yes, I, the Silver Ray, created the color spectrum from myself. Having all color within my silver, I was able to separate parts of my energy into a rainbow spectrum, one single color after another. (I say color, but sound and color go together.)

I call these colors (and sounds) subrays. Each of these subray colors is energy with a singular purpose. Seven subrays, seven purposes. Each subray that you perceive with your physical eyes has its own value, but it also has a Master assigned to it who is responsible for its power. These are the great Lords of Light. I gave birth to these rays and Lords of Light in a way similar to the Creator's own pattern of birthing life.

These great color subrays carry a particular aspect of God's being, through me, into the work of the many worlds. These subrays do not create physical matter themselves, but some of the Lords of Light have created low-level lifeforms. These Lords were all created primarily to assist in maintaining other creations. They are helpers of the highest type, which is why they carry designated titles such as Lords of Light. They energize that which they are directed to do to continue the plan of creation.

If we created a planet, a star, or a given star cluster, then we would designate a subray and its master to go to that area to support it according to its purpose in the plan. Thus, the Archangel Michael, connected with the Blue Ray, was C-ton's coordinator when the planet was ready for its first volunteer caretakers, and he was chosen because the blue ray carries the quality of scientific and technical understanding. Since the volunteers were doing what might be called biological and ecological caretaking, even the extension of certain botanical and zoological species, the color blue supported this type of activity. I will say more about C-ton's development later on.

I have indicated that you are a soul living in a physical body, and you have a guidance system of rays to express your soul's purpose throughout your life. Let me explain more about this from the beginning of your incarnation. In fact, return with me to the dimension you came from before birth. In that higher place you knew who you were, why you needed to come to Earth, and why you had chosen a particular set of rays as your spiritual guidance system.

When you were living in the higher dimensions, there was a thorough examination of your soul record with teachers and guides, in a type of spiritual evaluation. It was known that a number of cycles were to be completed for Earth caretakers and that there would be a massive cut-off between those who wished to respect God and those who did not.

You were told that you would have to conclude all of your past negative karma. In fact, you would need to gain self-mastery and balance for all prior Earth experiences. Moreover, you knew you had to stay clear enough that you would not get caught up in the negative vibrations of the planet itself, or in

66

the opinions of those who could cause you to waver from your self-determined path of completion. (Only a few souls came here totally free of past negativity, or karma, and were just offering themselves as helpers in a critical time.)

You were reminded that there are billions of people who were physical children of the "fallen" ones, or their later offspring, all of whom were finally granted souls and given an opportunity to complete self-mastery along with the first 11 million soul volunteers. So there would be billions to help assist Earth to her final glory. Regrettably, many have or will invite relationships with the dark forces in exchange for power and control, and these are truly evil ones, no matter their former soul status.

A part of this closing cycle, you were told, would allow all of the negative beings from the time of Atlantis to have a final replay of those infamous days, primarily as scientists who misused energy to the detriment of an entire human civilization, the planet, and the animal, plant, and mineral kingdoms. You knew before you came whether you had amends to make, to whom, and for what. One does not return without clarity and without the soul capacity of magnificence and commitment.

So you probably had a serious purpose for your entry onto the planet. Because you were told that you would be given guides, teachers, and a strong constellation of rays with a primary color of intention and several supplemental ones to help you complete your task, you came. The color choices were made according to negative karma, if any, and for support of the activities you needed for completion of self-mastery. With your evaluation committee's aid a choice of rays was made, and the opportunity to successfully balance all former experiences on Earth was approved.

But to enter the physical world remembering details of that 8-million-year Earth cycle would be too overwhelming. Thus, the veil descended over your memory.

You prepared for your last blindfolded journey.

When the couple whom you agreed to accept as parents gave birth, your threadlike soul entered the body. It was very small, this soul, to fit the infant size, but it grew rapidly, expanding and extending itself inside this physical chamber. Generally, the soul resides inside the *chest* cavity, but it might be in a higher or lower location for a few.

By the time you were 13 or 14, depending upon your state of awareness and consciousness of yourself as more than a body, you remembered what you came to do. Perhaps you planned to be a nurse, doctor, or healer of some kind, a lawyer or judge, a teacher or counselor, an inventor or engineer, artist, musician, farmer, poet or writer, businessman or minister, and so on. You had that goal to start from, and with this clarity, you began to carry out your soul intention.

Hopefully, you did not allow others to dissuade you from your own knowingness or prevent you from fulfilling your goal. Your job or vocation, though only one aspect of life, gives an avenue for meaningful service. It brings you to certain people, places, and activities of considerable importance.

As you reached adulthood the quality of your soul became more and more expressive. Most importantly, from 1986 onward, you knew that great spiritual energies would be sent to stimulate your ray colors by feeding you rainbow colors to match your own.

It is important to realize that the energy vibrations of the Great Rays descend toward the Earth in a rainfall fashion, not in a horizontal arc. Thus, you have a vertical relationship with them during the Time of Awakening, and since the rays extend three feet over your head, they can be easily nourished.

This brief description of how your soul and its rays are placed inside the body, and how it shares guidance through an inner knowing or conscience, should be encouraging. The critical point is that *your soul purpose is not the same as everyone else's!* Some people do not recognize this fact, as when an unawakened parent may try to force an offspring into a goal that really is not appropriate for the soul. In another situation a wonderful helpmate may sense what another is to do while that one has gotten lost in the maze of material forgetfulness, ignoring the soul's mission.

The major idea we can suggest is that *each person should be quiet every day to listen within.* Your soul purpose is contained inside, where it is always accessible to assist and direct you. But do you even talk to it?

How often we hear you of Earth complaining to God that you don't know what to do, yet you never slow down to find the answer within. Jesus, and others, said, "Be still."

Now I share the same advice. Be still.

Not only should you meditate daily, but it is very important that you join weekly with others like yourself. You can assist and care for one another and make the journey one of cooperation and peace. Consider this well. Let your soul guide you using its built-in colors of knowing. These rays are your guiding rudder, your special gift from the Silver Ray at this critical time.

We are often asked what happens to your ray when you die. Since you chose the particular ray constellation for this one life expression only, you are free of it upon the transition called death. You have not been on the same rays consistently.

Now it is appropriate to explain the ray colors to you in some detail. Although only I, or those Lords of Light working with me, can see them and describe them, you can feel their influence and sense or hear their inner assistance. Although some of your clairvoyant persons see the light *around* your body, which you call the aura, this is *not* the same thing. Your main ray is inside the physical vehicle but extends up above the body for three feet. The aura surrounds the body as a wider field of energy. Kindly do not confuse the two! You have both, but they are different. Some day those in human bodies will see them, and your photographers, scientists, physicians, or others may find a way to physically demonstrate their radiance.

Meanwhile, I will describe these colors to you for your edification. But in all things you must begin to ask your own consciousness, within, about your soul purpose, if you are in doubt. For the clarity of your purpose can be given to you whether you see your rays or not. I repeat: Meditate. Be silent. Ask within. It is possible for any serious human of goodwill to develop spiritually through willingness and discipline.

Remember that C-ton is the only planet in creation where all seven colors of the rainbow spectrum can be seen simultaneously. In fact, most planets have only one or two, and having many colors makes our work more difficult! This visual delight and full-of-wonder experience is my gift. Use it in your darkened world where you have fallen into the blind forgetfulness of near spiritual annihilation. These colors were given so you could choose and appreciate color in a variety of wonderful substances.

Neither do all levels or *dimensions* use the same colors. Two colors seen on Earth as red and orange are not needed at the fourth dimensional level. While you need the push and vitality of red for accomplishment and the spiritual vision of orange for connection with higher vibratory realms, these colors are not necessary beyond the third dimension.

If you have studied artistic subjects, you are aware of the different saturations and values that colors contain. You know that the addition of darker shades can create different subcolors, murkiness, and so on. The same is true if you add white or a lighter color. We use each energy color as purely as possible in your ray structure so its brilliance will not fade or change; nevertheless, within the color green are many shades of green. Once your shade is selected, it does not tend to change.

However, if you are destructive to yourself through negative thinking and physical violence, you can muddy or distort the original soul and ray radiance. Conversely, if you are meditating, praying, contemplating, and communing with the soul-of-you, other meditators, guides, and teachers, it can be brightened and made more glowing. You would never go from one major color to another, however, such as from blue to yellow.

A handful of humans have almost a white ray of purity and appear to have a halo effect about them. These sages, saints, avatars, masters, and so on, have usually devoted their lives to inner purification and are then witnessed in this whiter, brighter aspect of self. Also, some of them came upon either a silver or gold ray in the beginning that glistens radiantly in its natural unpolluted condition.

Are you interested in knowing more about the meaning of the colors in your rainbow spectrum? In your own ray structure?

RAY COLORS
RED
This color is the most energetic or vitalizing of all the spectrum. It pushes people into action, so those who have it are energetic and full of life. This "drive-to-get-things-done" ray is often chosen by a soul as its ray of intention if it has previously been shy, hesitant, lazy, fearful, or unwilling to fulfill its responsibilities to the God forces and the planet. Just as the vitality of the blood flowing through the human body is a circu-

latory system, the red ray circulates new energy and gives persistence of expression. These red ray people are usually undaunted by major tasks and proceed with enthusiasm, often without exhaustion, when others must rest or quit. They are the doers par excellence. If this red color is the soul's ray of intention, rather than one of the supplemental rays next to the primary one, personal energy will be consistently vibrant for chosen tasks. This high energy person will get the job done, but not necessarily with gentleness, patience, and compassion.

When souls add white or silver to their red ray and choose to enter life on a *pink* or love ray, they can be the epitome of love in a human body. If they do not become "door mats" or recluses, they can make a major contribution just by their presence. They contribute just by be-ing.

Those on the pink ray care deeply about serving others. Their energy is peaceful and helpful under most circumstances, and their motives are seldom self-centered. They are the great givers of time and energy to whatever they undertake, for part of their ray color still has the push and vitality of red.

The planet is blessed by these who can accomplish service with a rosy beauty, for these are the emotional love fountains needed for peace and to help balance those on blue rays. Due to the pink ray's great sensitivity, they can feel rejected easily and must learn some detachment in human relationships. For some souls the choice of pink is an opportunity to reclaim balance in a soul long overpowered with intellect and lack of concern about others. For those without negative karma, it is frequently the ray chosen to assist the planet and help balance its many problems.

ORANGE
Orange is the color of the unseen kingdoms. It allows a human to be interested in, and concerned with, activities of the

72

spiritual realms, particularly as it relates to the elemental, devic, and angelic realms. It is these invisible ones who assist in the protection and guidance of the Earth itself and the plant kingdom. Contrary to popular opinion, there really are invisible helpers of many sizes and types that attend and guide kingdoms other than human. Clairvoyant humans can sometimes see these fascinating lifeforms, called by such names as fairies and angels. These angelic creations were needed after the original human caretakers fell into unconsciousness and were no longer capable of, or interested in, maintaining plant life or the conditions of the planet itself. These invisible ones are the mammoth team who were brought to replace the original caretakers and are still here for planetary care. Orange is very rare as a primary ray and even infrequent as a supplemental ray. Those on orange have windows into the true reality of life and are very sensitive bridges to spiritual forces.

YELLOW

Animals were created as the companions for humans after the souls "fell" from their higher light vibration. It is regrettable that many people have mistreated animals during their innumerable Earth experiences. Killing animals for food is generally not the reason karmic restitution must be made to them, however. The negative cause is most likely constant physical abuse or a hunter's pride-in-trophies that troubles a soul when later reviewing its lifestream experience out-of-body. Killing the animals of the wild for food is reviewed differently than killing the handsomest animal specimen for reasons of pride or beating horses to death and so on.

Domesticated animals are more defenseless than some jungle creatures and are frequently tortured or neglected, even today. Your technical laboratories collect, and eventually kill through experimentations for the "good of humans," a variety of the smaller creations from mice to guinea pigs and rabbits. While society considers human life more valuable than that of a tiny creation, be advised that the entire planet is an interconnected link of life that must work together. To kill creatures indifferently raises a serious question about the compassionate quality of a soul. If you must kill a defenseless creature that is not endangering your own life, at least honor its life by sending love or respect. In doing this you may avoid much soul grief at a later time. I caution you that dominion does not give you license to abuse life or kill without reason and compassion.

Those who experience the deep love for a domestic animal or bird, and who demonstrate this by concern and dedication, are often viewed by others—if they become too involved—as a little "weird." This is not to deny that some people do carry their affection to ridiculous measures, but the love aspect of a human being is often nourished by caring for something smaller and more helpless. Since animals, even birds, are voiceless (though they make understandable sounds), they cannot vocalize any extensive message. They are here, then, to communicate unconditional love as a non-verbal expression. Humans may be judgmental and unaccepting to one another for a variety of emotional reasons, but domesticated animals have an outstanding record of continuous devotion.

Some humans must care for these less able ones and teach them that love can be reciprocated, and it is this concept that the yellow ray allows a human soul to experience and claim for its truth.

Those on the yellow ray are often seen observing and watching the animals, protecting them, and taking legal action on their behalf, if necessary. They express respect for an animal's soul and appreciate the individualized expression of each lifeform. Let your heart open to the understanding that the true meaning of the word dominion is *caretaker*.

GREEN

Although the planet was originally light blue, over eons of time that hue was softened to green, which is the primary color of growing things on your planet now. Green trees, grass, shrubs, plants, and voluminous flowers give a beauty that is unmistakably C-ton. But green represents more than these plant forms; green is the color for Mother Earth herself. Green denotes total respect and concern for the planet and all life upon it. It is soul appreciation at the deepest level. Green ray people are attempting to bring conservation into practice so the pollution and damage done to the Earth can be healed. Green ray people are capable of great nurturing and are especially needed in your century when so much land is being destroyed, so many trees cut, and so many green things decimated.

Those souls who came on the green ray are often gardeners or involved in landscaping and beautification of the planet. They may also have interest in ecology, conservation. Others have interest in physical and emotional healing of humans and animals. Many medical people, especially holistic health practitioners, who use herbs and natural healing approaches—such as color and energy—come on the green ray.

Many of the beings who enter upon the green ray have either come as free, non-karmic souls with a deep love for Earth, or have caused serious problems to Earth in the past, particularly in the days of Atlantis. Some are here to make restitution, then, but others came voluntarily to prevent further ignorance, irresponsibility, and devastation. Dominion means being responsible; this is the green ray's gift.

BLUE

The blue ray of soul intention on planet Earth at this time represents high mental acuity, technological and scientific interests, and intellectual comprehension, whether the being actually works in a laboratory or not. Even if a blue ray soul follows other interests, its logic will make it good at problem-solving. The blue ray soul is often considered an unemotional individual without compassion or love. Yet, a blue ray soul *can* care. Those who follow an analytical inquiry to its limits for a *positive* solution are greatly needed in your world today, for you are beset with major problems that true science could resolve.

Those on the blue ray of soul intention must be particularly aware that their knowledge and power must demonstrate respect toward God and universal laws. Cosmic principles must not be misused for any reason, and the use of the intellect for creating weaponry and destructive materials is prohibited.

In Atlantis many beings of high intellect created horrendous weapons for personal power and glorification, and they are here in huge numbers, as a parallel experience, to replay that former period to the advantage of society this time, not to its detriment.

Nonetheless, some scientific and intellectual beings are already repeating their destructiveness in the creation of hydrogen, nuclear, and atomic weapons and instruments. Therefore, society must prevent any further insanity and intellectual arrogance on its part.

Those most recalcitrant Atlantean souls who begged for mercy, and have been allowed a final opportunity to serve God's forces, were given an added touch of spiritual discernment and cosmic wisdom to their blue ray before they entered this life pattern, but of course, each soul has free will once it arrives in the body.

Because true science is the discovery and application of universal laws and principles for the betterment of all life, the blue ray has special responsibility here. In this life it is to use cosmic energy for peaceful, constructive purposes in whatever area of work is chosen. Misuses of energy for negative warlike goals will bring swift karmic justice. Conservation, protection, and reclamation for the atmosphere, the waters, all life contained in the waters, and neutralization of toxic wastes especially needs blue ray assistance. In its highest octave, intelligence leads life towards the First Cause or spiritual form. When used for this purpose a blue ray soul serves admirably and completes its soul purpose.

INDIGO

Although this color seems to be unique, it is presently a part of the blue ray until its real meaning is brought to Earth by a great master. Indigo, or midnight navy blue, is the color of cosmic space which God has created, and so we do not consider it a separate ray. Few people have this navy blue soul color, but those who do will have inter-galactic connections and stellar relationships in this lifetime. They can be communication links between space beings and your own human family. Their one requirement is to become *spiritually* grounded and committed to the Creator before opening themselves to a position of association with other lifeforms, whether in your own solar system, galaxy, or universe.

Many of these souls enjoy studying the stars because it brings a soul sense of reconnection to other places that also have lifeforms and existence.

VIOLET or PURPLE

During the Time of Awakening upon your planet, this ray was designated as the representative, or ambassador, of spiritual peace. Its main soul intention desires personal harmony, group cooperation, and the relinquishment of weapons. This ray leads to the understanding and expression of harmonious living as a true life commitment. Spiritual togetherness is based on love and caring; therefore peace, true peace, is prompted by a feeling of oneness.

Souls who come on a purple peace ray are here to bring individual (inner) peace in balance with world (outer) peace. This may be centered at home, in organizations and institutions, but also among nations, internationally, where peaceful expression and cooperation are a growing necessity.

Some upon this ray are free souls who have come to make a much needed contribution to change the planet. Some, as you might surmise, are here to balance former hateful, violent actions and bring life to a higher level of peace on Earth.

OTHER RAYS

Brown, a combination of red and purple, presently signifies a confusion or motivation problem when it is seen as a thin band in a soul ray constellation. Generally weak and pale in hue, brown is the only color that can be changed or removed. One day soon, brown will have a higher meaning and will eventually be used as a ray to introduce *total awareness of the interior of the planet*. This color will be rich and vibrant to accomplish its purpose.

The *X-ray*, which is able to see beyond apparent reality or existence, can perceive other dimensions within, or relating to, *matter*. *Infra-red* is similar to this and is able to see inherent life energies within matter. *Ultra-violet* is yet another ray situated in the invisible spectrum.

Now all of these so-called invisible rays were given to show you the true reality. You frequently have been told that your Earth life is the illusion and that which is unseen is the genuine reality. We prefer to use a more accurate term, "all-is-existence," rather than illusion, because even the illusion is an existence of lower form vibration.

Now, there is no white ray, per se, but there is white light. Many of you equate this white light with the God force energy, but we call it life energy, or life power. It is an almost color-less energy that contains positive and negative electrons that vibrate rapidly at a rate determined by the unique properties of other physical objects. In some respects it is the same as a blank piece of paper—the beginningness of anything. It also can fully absorb the God force energy without interference by other color rays.

You will find that there are sometimes overlappings or in-termingling of colors into ray combinations, such as blue-green.

The rays also have dilutions or intensifications caused by adding or combining a color or light that works with it very closely. These others are usually silver, gold, or white light. These additions change the *emphasis* of the original ray, such as red to pink or red to ruby. The red is pure vitality or the push of human energy, whereas the pink embodies the push but is softened to concern for the human being. Blue contains technical and scientific intellect, yet it has been softened with a silver or a white aspect for cosmic discernment and spiritual wisdom this lifetime.

In all things the intensity or depth of the ray color is related to the vibratory intensity and longing of the soul.

I have left the *gold* and *silver* soul rays to the last because there are very few of these on your planet; however, their influ-ence is critical during this Time of Awakening. Some 4,000 souls with silver as their ray of intention are situated some-where in the western states of America now and have not yet awakened. They should come forth immediately to accept their soul responsibility for preservation of all life, peace on Earth.

Those who came upon the silver soul ray are naturally aware of the cosmic forces and creations beyond your planet.

They can express that life is more than what you see and clarify the need for protecting both cosmic and creative energies.

The strong souls who are here upon the gold ray of intention are expressions of God's will and power and usually come to teach the necessity of following universal laws and principles in all things. They grasp the fundamentals of a cooperative universe and the interrelationship of all life essences. Those on the gold soul ray lead and guide a faltering humanity toward universal good. They respect the concept of cosmic responsibility and revere the One that brought all life into existence, that now calls humanity to build a global society in which peace is a reality.

Are there any questions you wish to ask about this material?

QUESTIONS BY VIRGINIA ESSENE TO SILVER RAY
(Ann Valentin entranced)

V.   Could you start at the very beginning? How do we get our rays in this Time of Awakening?

S.R.   The ray comes with the soul and is like a thin energy thread, almost invisible. The soul carries it along when it comes into the body.

V.   When does the soul's ray of intention become activated?

S.R.   When the baby emerges into the world. It has been assigned to the life energy while in the womb, you see.

V.   This is not the silver cord?

S.R.   No. When the infant is born on your plane the "thread" starts to grow and expand. As the child grows physically, the ray unwinds and multiplies or matures with the being. As the person becomes adult, the ray then extends above the head so that it is relating to the invisible energies that are *outside* the physical body. The tightly compacted radiances reach full size at approximately 28 years of age and are glorious to watch. When I view your body, the rays show me your essence, and I can give a soul reading. Persons are usually aware of their soul intention by age fourteen, whether the personality follows through with it or not.

V.   You have used the term "soul storage." Could you explain that, please?

S.R.   Roughly 6 million years ago, when souls were placed in physical bodies, death began, and so reincarnation became a temporary necessity until souls could complete their original contracts. When they first reincarnated, they didn't have a ray of intention connected to the soul. They just came back into the body with the soul inside. Other spiritual beings guided them, of course, but there were no *inner rays*. So the soul was in storage, so to speak. The ray of intention gift was instituted to get you out of "soul storage" by changing humanity's behavior and the evolutionary path of the planet very quickly. We urgently wish each soul to complete its contract as an Earth caretaker, to attain its mastery, and then return to its original home, go to another dominion or location, or choose to stay upon Earth at a higher state of consciousness.

V.   Do you have any last comments about the rays we humans have?

S.R.   Our attempt to describe something you have never seen is difficult, and my remarks probably carry insufficient impact. But try to imagine that you can see your soul inside your chest and its ray of intention moving out the top of your skull. Then visualize the rainbow colors totally surrounding your planet, showering hues and radiance into the very depths of your being. Your soul is being transfused with color vibration at a rapid rate to assist your awakening from spiritual amnesia and illusion.

If you have ever watered your garden and watched a magnificent rosebush drink deeply to sustain itself, perhaps you can perceive our joy in giving you spiritual sustenance so that your own soul's life beauty can grow, mature, bloom.

You are the caretakers of this earthly garden, but you have been asleep. May we count on your consistent willingness to awaken to your responsibility so the planet finally reaches its Time of Radiance? For this was your original contract those 8 million years ago (or since then as a newer soul.) Let us join together in a task long overdue and bring *peace on Earth*. Regardless of when your soul was created, please join the divine plan. All are welcome. All are needed.

We send our radiant, celestial colors to cheer you and lead you boldly through darkness to victory's blazing light. Oh, caretakers, oh, caretakers, oh, caretakers ... you are called forth by your creators.

It is time, now, to accomplish your goal.

Chapter VI

You and Your Planet

All of life is related. You, the planet itself, and all living things are one interwoven design intended for harmony and balance. You cannot change the design, but you can understand it, support and care for its many facets, and thus achieve mastery of this level of existence. This is your challenge that we assist with in this urgent hour. There are no exemptions to your role here as caretakers.

Humanity's present position in the spiritual evolution is like a springtime day. Our energy vibrations melt the snow of your sleep, warm and give momentum to your personal growth. There will now be an awareness that spring is upon the soul of each person. Even as the Sun warms the air, bringing growth within the trees, our rays stimulate your essence. Your season of growth is here.

This season of spiritual change bursts forth with the urgent vitality of its original nature, renewing the hillsides, the fields, the grass ... and *you*! You are presently aware that the potential growth of your own life consciousness, which has always been there, is blossoming, also.

Now the necessary ingredients for all physical life on Earth are air and moisture. All living things need water. The fluid of your body is water based even as the fluid for the land is water.

But life is also light, color, and sound. This spiritual life is another aspect reflected in nature and you as well. Your planet is a planet of color. You vibrate with and to color.

When you look at the flowers, trees, animals, birds, and sea life, notice their colors and the uniqueness of their design. Each item has been created like a finely tuned instrument to give you enjoyment, healing, and to remind you of the spiritual aspect of life. Never doubt there is something behind all things far beyond the physical. It is the spiritual essence of God, the First Cause, that should be perceived in all that has been created. During this Time of Awakening we are accelerating the understanding of how color can *heal* you emotionally and physically. As you discover the importance of colors as they relate to your rays, your wellbeing, enthusiasm, and emotions will improve.

It is vital for you to understand that your planet is *green* and *water-dependent.* You do not want to become another Mars! All of the plant life that sustains your planet needs water and begins with a green content, bursting forth from the soil with a green stem and/or pod. The plant kingdom, which was created to feed animal and human life and gladly serves you to this end, is green. When you thank and bless any green thing for its goodness, the cycle is complete without karma to you for destroying it.

Intricate in design, useful, fascinating, and beautiful, everything here is for your enjoyment or to aid your physical, emotional, and spiritual wellbeing. Water and air, a tree, a flower, a rock, the soil, an animal, a whale, your pet dog, that horse you like—each thing is here for a purpose. *Nothing is random.*

You are to respect life creations that do not have souls as the humans and animals do. Although your body is a creation of wonder, you are not the end result of life here. The human personality is still imperfect. Work on yourself as a *part* of the planet's lifestream, and retain some humility.

Beyond their physical attractiveness and purpose, each creation in our design has a higher intention, most of which you have forgotten or neglected.

For example, you and plants have a symbiotic relationship. Oxygen and carbon dioxide exchanges must go on to preserve all life. Yet some trees are dying from the smog and cannot give back the oxygen that you need. Others are cut down without reforestation; consequently, the number of trees is constantly diminishing. What will your world do if steps are not taken to preserve the trees and prohibit the pollution of your air?

From space, the most noticeable aspect of your planet is probably its glistening blue waters and white cloud cover. You still have more surface water than any place in your solar system; nevertheless, not all of it can be drunk because these fresh waters are becoming polluted, just like your atmosphere. The air you breathe is tainted. The air and water dependency aspects of your planet were planned as part of an *interrelated unit*, and if you defile them, the entire life chain on Earth will be greatly imbalanced, possibly damaged beyond your repair. You must preserve these vital elements for your survival.

Not only are the fresh water supplies being poisoned, but now even the great oceans are being filled with enormous amounts of toxic materials, particularly radioactive, atomic, nuclear, and even hydrogen wastes. This is insanity. Humans do not understand our concern because the oceans are so vast that they seem invulnerable to a few things being "tossed" there. Your governments dump the worst things they possess either into the Earth or the oceans. And you, dweller of C-ton, apparently do not realize the danger.

Let us think together a moment. What living things abide in that area you call sea or ocean?

Perhaps you say "fish," "whales," "dolphins," "otters," "seals," and so forth. All deserve a clean, safe place to reside, do they not? Also acknowledge the importance of whales and dolphins to the human species. First, they are mammal cousins. Second, they are an information source about what is happening to the interior of your planet, which is badly ruptured due to the hydrogen and other underground nuclear explosions your governments set off.

Through their sonar abilities these behemoths, the whales, and the friendly schools of dolphins and porpoises, are able to monitor the activity of Earth's geological plates and ascertain information about potential Earth movement. Accept that these "friends" must be protected because they are living things, and also because we need their sonar reports, which are monitored by our staff in space. Your submarines either cannot do this monitoring task with coverage underneath all the seas, or you humans will not cooperate on the project. It is sad that humans know very little about the oceans and what their true meaning is.

In fact, since you know so little about the design of this planet, we have come now, so that the condition can be rectified, and you can quickly accept your responsibilities to preserve all life upon it.

The trees that you enjoy are here for specific purposes. The evergreen trees that, regardless of weather changes, stay green to heal the planet, take the negative vibrations from those loud, angry words that you speak, and neutralize them. They harmonize energy. While all trees absorb some sound and negativity, it is primarily the evergreen trees that are working with the healing of the planet itself, which is a living thing. Since energy curves, you will find evergreen trees around the entire globe unless you have destroyed them.

The magnificent redwood and cedar trees, tall and majestic, reddish in tint, are designated to heal the heart and lung regions of humans and animals. The difference between a cedar and a redwood tree is the *radius* of the beam of healing energy that comes from the tree. From a cedar it fans out, whereas a redwood tree has a direct beam. This is why, when you are in the cedars or redwoods, you feel healed and peaceful, for you are tuning into the vibrations of the trees themselves. You are awed by their magnificence, but you are also being healed at the same time. If you need to be strengthened in these bodily areas you can go there and be among these trees. Fifteen minutes to two hours in their presence in a meditative state, a receptive state, will bring peace from their healing energies. Although these healing properties continue for about a two year period after the tree is cut down, their vibrations are greatly lessened. After that time you may have an object of beauty or usefulness, but it no longer contains any healing vibrations.

Oak trees are designated to work with the spine and the strength of the back muscles. If you need to heal the back areas, it is recommended that you sit with your back against the oak tree, while it is still living. Then you feel its vitality and strength as it gathers energy from the soil and air. As an oak reaches its mighty branches out into space, it exemplifies your own position of rootedness on the planet while reaching to the heavens.

Teakwood trees help heal brain disorders, headaches, or anything so related. And madrones assist the neck area if you approach within eight to twelve inches for a sustained period.

Eucalyptus trees focus on the lungs, bronchials, sinuses, nostrils—all that relates to the breathing apparatus. Reaching high into the air, they remind you to stand upright, breathe strongly, and hold your head up, so that you are aware of the air and the sunlight.

Besides trees we have collected many plants from throughout the galaxies of this universe and scientifically adapted them for your planet. The first soul rays who came as caretakers were assistants in this process. For example, what you have called the aloe plant is known in the stellar regions as the aum plant. This aum plant came to Venus and Saturn in your solar system from the western region of your universe. In all places it is used for its healing properties to the interior, as well as the exterior, of any lifeform. It has properties of rejuvenation and helps the human body maintain the cell vitality.

Each plant that is here was brought to sustain your life by giving you food and medicine or to anchor the soil so it does not blow away with the winds. Our purpose for your planet was that the entire globe should be a garden. Yes, I understand that you find this difficult to believe as you see great desert areas, but even your recorded history will tell you that many of these places were once green. Some areas, particularly that which you have noted as Africa, have been greatly changed through past warfare.

Over thousands of years the trees have been cut down and the plants dug up, leaving nothing to hold moisture. Then, as soon as the Sun beat down, the land dried up. But these deserts can be reclaimed when water is brought in, and we intend during the next 22 to 25 years to release new technology to assist this project. This action will help balance the entire globe so the deserts will bloom again, and your populace will move about and be in all places, not just congregated in large cities. You will again enjoy the land and be in harmony with it.

You each can have your own space to live in, even as you work with your fellow humans and feel a closeness with the Earth itself. The entire planet is to be inhabited eventually.

Only the polar caps are not to be fully utilized for living conditions at this time. They are pressure points holding the physical crusts or geological plates in a tight compactness to even out pressures that are in the Earth's interior.

The oceans have many aspects to them, but a primary purpose is to assist with the water cycle by putting moisture into the air. As the moisture moves about, it gives you rain to water the plants and provides drinking water to survive. We have already discussed your ocean survival team called dolphins, porpoises, and whales, which are a communication system, reporting to us the physical danger from interior Earth movements.

Within your oceans are fish that you are now using for food, but you are beginning to understand that the oceans have plant substances that can give you food and sustain you very easily, in small amounts, with vitality and vigor. The plants or food substances that come from the ocean will allow you *keener intelligence.* As they are not heavy food, they will supply increased vibrations to the cells and allow you a richer combination of oxygen within the blood. This oxygenation gives a more perceptive thought process so that you feel more physically vital and mentally alert.

The product you call spirulina is an earlier aspect of the germanium, and it contains the vitality just mentioned. The newer products will have an even higher rate of vitality. They will be refined even more, eventually, so that the ultimate food for a human can come from the oceans. If this research is completed, you will truly be able to eat smaller amounts of food and yet sustain or increase your vitality at least 22 percent.

Now, what about rocks? Why did we create them? Why do you pick up a rock when you go someplace and perhaps put it in your pocket or lug it for miles? Because it soothes you by removing negative vibrations. Have you ever held a small rock in your hand, tossed it around, back and forth? It makes you feel good. They are more than you suspect, these bountiful rocks, which is why there are so many. You need these apparently useless things for more than mere building materials.

Now besides being available as outdoor seating, big rocks are also soothers. When you go to a beautiful place with a view, you want to sit on a rock, sometimes for a long time. Rocks are comforting; beige or light grey rocks are most active in relieving negative vibrations. Have them in your garden, or around your feet when you meditate. Indoors you can just have them in your house to absorb negative vibrations because they are like a little factory. In two hours they can usually put positive vibrations back into the atmosphere. If the vibrations are quite negative however, it takes years.

Have you ever really looked at soil, especially its color and texture? It is receptive and is now releasing physical and spiritual vibrations, both upward and downward. Colors are pertinent to the type of soil and its amplification qualities, and we will release more data when this knowledge is needed. The soils, too, are awakening.

Now what you call the animals, whether they be on land or in the waters, are here primarily as your companions. We have given you immense *variety*. You have your affectionate playmates called pets and the undomesticated or wild species. Before "the fall," or course, you were the caretakers of some of these same animals. Since acquiring a human form, however, they are your fellow Earth dwellers, and you have an entire animal family to relate to. For the human body was designed to be with these other lifeforms—not only animals, but also the fowl, plants, trees, and so on.

The intent of life on this planet is companionship and benign relationships among the species. All creatures, even the animals, were to be vegetarian and non-harmful to others. Can your mind even grasp a planet like that? Can you see a lion chewing hard-shell nuts rather than flesh? That is truly what the sharp teeth were for. Everything is perception, is it not?

Due to humanity's intrusion into animal habitats for war or so-called "development," these vegetarian creations have become cannibalistic, or carnivorous. Many are now ferocious beasts in need of harmonious balance again. But this was not meant to be. In fact, we brought the felines to C-ton from planet Uranus with only minor adaptations. Others, like the ape/gorilla family, we brought from a planet 12 galaxies away. This is why we are almost amused at your attempts to link human evolution to apes. We created you first and brought them here afterwards for companionship.

We are often asked why we created poisonous snakes, and the answer is simple. They were not poisonous in the beginning. They dug tunnels to a depth of some eight feet for irrigation, even as the crocodiles helped with irrigation by moving through stagnant water to bring freshness and to allow sunlight and growth to occur more vigorously.

I remind you once again that all things are part of our planetary master plan, but the plan has long since become imbalanced. All things were here for a purpose. In the future we will use frequency vibration to undo negative instinctual behaviors, even as your own vibrations are being raised into higher consciousness by color. These ideas may be beyond your comprehension for the moment, but humanity is on the threshold of miraculous progress. Only your willingness to think new thoughts and entertain novel ideas is necessary.

With your assistance the future is bright, and Earth will become radiant and peaceful as it was in the beginning.

Just like animals and plants, gemstones are also living things but of denser vibration or solidity. They were created with internal healing properties. It is important you understand that these colored gemstones are *alive and can conduct energy*. This ability means they can give and receive. Therefore, you should not constantly wear gemstones in the throat area, over the heart, or below the waist.

Crystals are beautiful, but you must be careful in their use. I speak of quartz crystals which are extremely powerful. It is recommended that you *not* wear a quartz crystal for more than six hours at a time because they can affect the rate of your heartbeat. You are a vibratory being, and the impulses are picked up by the quartz. Humans put crystals in radios and transmitters for this very reason. They never stop resonating! If you have crystals in your bedroom, cover them up at night or put them in something wooden, if possible, so they are not actively vibrating where you are. Because amethyst is also very powerful and has the same properties, the same warning applies. Your sleeptime should be a time for rest and healing, a time when your heartbeat slows down, a time to totally relax and let healing take place within your body. Since it is also a time for soul learning, training, and sometimes travel, it should *not* be influenced by impulses from quartz crystals. The best use of crystals is during meditation when strong impulses are desired or for specified healing practices.

It is helpful to remember that the reason most people are drawn to crystals now is because there is a remembrance of Atlantis where crystals were everywhere. Crystals eventually caused the downfall of Atlantis, in fact. A giant crystal over the land was giving off beams to the land itself, causing overload. Many humans are here who misused crystals then by programming them for personal power and control over others. You are to understand that a crystal can be programmed; you can put your thoughts into it. In this Time of Awakening crystals are to be kept as healing tools, for meditation, or other positive purposes. Serious karmic consequences will accrue for their misuse again.

Now, are there questions you would ask?

QUESTIONS BY VIRGINIA ESSENE TO SILVER RAY
(Ann Valentin entranced)

V.   Silver Ray, if people are supposed to be eating food from the oceans, why did you provide all the fruit trees, seeds, nuts, vegetables, and grains of the soil to feed people?

S.R.   This is a balancing factor so that as the spiritual awakening becomes more evident and the human intelligence increases, ocean substances will make up 22 percent of food intake. Eventually, it would be perhaps 47 percent of your substance. The remainder of intake would be balanced with the products of the Earth itself. You may have the water products—what you term hydroponics—as well as the Earth or soil products.

V.   Given that Earth foods and animal and fish flesh constitute the majority of the human diet, how do you expect this change to ocean food to occur? Will people adapt to a different texture and taste?

S.R.   An educational program is needed so they will accept the *vitality* of these substances. The flavor can be enhanced by adding different ingredients. In all things you have your creative imagination to assist you.

V.   If fish were not meant to be eaten, why are there so many species of fish?

S.R.   The species of fish were given for beauty and interest, like birds you enjoy. It was, and is, part of the original Earth plan for cities to be within and above the oceans. So just as in the air you see multicolored birds, in the oceans you can observe multicolored fish for you pleasure. You have fish bowls now; why not an ocean bowl?

V.   You are speaking of actual cities beneath the ocean?

S.R.   Yes. There was a small one, but the ultimate plan has not been fully utilized.

V.   Since people have lungs to breathe air, why would you put them under the ocean?

S.R.   For total usage of the planet. It is just a different aspect of existence. We thought you might like to be down there to see it.

V.   It is very dark down there.

S.R.   But we have plans so it wouldn't be dark. You have not even perceived the possible technical marvels of life in the Time of Radiance. You are not going to be just stuck in certain little areas. Have you ever seen a drop of water from the ocean? It has the same colors of the spectrum as your rainbows.

V.   Yes, I have seen that. You mentioned having cities above the water? What does that mean?

S.R.   We were going to have floating cities. Remember, you came to Earth as caretakers, so we are not going to have you in space until you have fulfilled your contract here. Until peace comes, we wish you to be earthbound and take care of the Earth while part of it. We wish you to be in harmony with it and enjoy it. The ultimate plan for you and Earth is extremely pleasurable. You will be very happy! And I tell you that it will soon happen!

V.   If people need the Sun, why would they live under water?

S.R.   For a novel experience, just as you like to go on vacations and try something different; wouldn't you like to try living beneath the ocean for a while? It is very beautiful there.

V.   I confess to some personal fear about living underwater. It is dangerous there in case anything leaks.

S.R. In all things you have free will and choice, but I assure you we have metals that you don't even know about. The metals that are used in spaceships would be very adaptable and safe for it. We have not even begun to give you all of the technical advances that will enhance your future because much of any information you now receive is still used for destructive purposes. When your true soul intelligence can be turned to the preservation of all life, we will open new channels of true scientific development.

V. Speak more about the birds, please.

S.R. The birds are here for your physical enjoyment; they give you laughter, joy, beauty, music. Birds do not have souls; they are created with what you term instinct. Insects are soulless things, of course.

V. You created insects so the birds would have food?

S.R. No, that is an out-of-balance factor that has come upon your planet. Insects have an occupation to help plants grow; they also aerate the soil itself by pollinating.

V. Why are there such wide varieties among birds? Huge things like ostriches who can't fly at all, and then other birds that can soar and swoop?

S.R. Those were created just to bring different experiences. Each thing does not necessarily have a specific purpose to maintain your life cycle. It may be here to bring you humor, joy, beauty, or grace of movement. All things are here for a purpose, but not necessarily a serious, dramatic purpose.

V. What about the undesirable things, like poisonous snakes, flies, mosquitoes?

S.R. At this particular time, and for at least 150 more years of your existence, they will be teaching you tolerance. Within this time, if you find it necessary to kill one of these things, so be it. You are not perfect, and we do not expect you to go around thinking you are. Since you are on an evolutionary pathway, we recommend you ask the deva that is involved with these pesty things to move them elsewhere. Tell the deva, or unseen helper who watches over plants, insects, and such soulless things, that by a certain time you will take action against them, unless they leave, because they are causing you discomfort. I am trying to tell you that if you find it necessary to smack a little bug then you do it with no guilt, but do not do it as your *first intention*. Seek first to get rid of the little creature peacefully. Warn it to go away, or go elsewhere, first; do not be so quick to snuff it out. We encourage humans to attune to the elementals and the devic helpers as much as possible. Once, long ago, some of you assisted with these Earth tasks before your fall into unconsciousness, but we had to bring a replacement program to care for planetary lifeforms when you caretakers were unavailable. At any rate, begin to appreciate how nature really works. A myriad of activities goes on right before your eyes, yet you are blind to the truth.

V.   Can you say more about the animals?

S.R.   The animals are soul creatures similar to humans. They are "voiceless ones" or silent ones, even though some make noises. They have chosen to be here. You have the domestic or home animals to work with you, comfort you, and give you companionship. Almost all pets give you unconditional love. Many times an animal takes the frustrations that you have—the angers, or whatever is difficult for you—accepts them and doesn't ever hate you. It doesn't judge or think you are not a nice person. An animal accepts your affection, appreciates it, and helps you express your human emotions so that you can find emotional balance within yourself.

V.   Did you say the "big cats" were not created to kill?

S.R.   Right. Their long teeth and big claws were for chewing certain branches of trees and eating nuts and fruits. In fact, all carnivorous animals were at one time vegetarians.

They were not created to be killers. Since their original creation, however, which has been distorted through eons of time, some are now harmful. In their natural habitat they would never have harmed humans and smaller animals. What I am saying, about life, is that certain things were created at certain times for certain purposes. Because of ignorance you view it as a meaningless jigsaw puzzle, and its fragments leave you confused. That is why we are here—to bring the light of truth.

V. What was the criterion for creating the gem and mineral kingdom? Were they all soulless?

S.R. Correct. None have souls. They are here merely to provide humanity with a means for *amplification of energies*, when needed. Consequently, these stones are available in the Earth, though not always obvious or evident to a human looking only at Earth's surface. In this Time of Awakening we will make known the importance of these gemstones. Now you can all use them to work with energy vibration amplification to help the soul on its rapid evolution.

V. But weren't gems and minerals already used in many past civilizations for healing?

S.R. Yes, but only by a few people. Now they will be used by millions of people.

V. So this is a mass utilization, rather than keeping gems for those who can afford it?

S.R. Yes. Many of the ancient ones who knew about these stones kept the information secret; it is not to be secret now.

V. How do you expect people to behave themselves and not loot these things or steal them from one another, even kill to have them as valuable possessions, as they have done in the past?

S.R. Because there are many of these stones around, and they are to be used in everyday work, not just as jewelry. There is not to be a high financial value put on them by faceting and beautification. Stones are valuable for their natural color. The secret of your future vitality, of healing, is *color*. All natural colored stones will be useful and should be available to everyone.

V.   How will people be able to identify what kind of a stone they should use without years or months of education?

S.R.   They will hold it in their hands. They will pick it up in their left hand, feel it, and then put it in their right hand. They will know by a personal vibration experience.

V.   Since most people today don't feel vibrations, how do you expect this to change?

S.R.   All people are now beginning to be aware of our increased acceleration of Earth time. A year from now when the 20 percent vibratory increase has occurred, they will be able to feel energy vibrations of many kinds.

V.   Are you saying that this ability is going to become automatic and unconscious?

S.R.   Yes. It has to do with the vibrations of the colors of the rainbow that are being amplified around your planet. I wish to complete this topic in greater detail, please, before we close the chapter.

The mineral kingdom is one of our greatest gifts to you, but it is generally misunderstood by your population. Gemstones have gone through chemical changes to be *concentrated energies*. These stones that you call gemstones, meaning stones with financial value, are valuable to us only because they have colors containing the vibrations that relate to your *soul rays*. As additional information comes out during this Time of Awakening about their true essence and as the vibrations upon the planet are increased, the relationship of each person to gemstones, even unpolished stones, will be enhanced.

As your understanding of working with colors to heal the physical body and the emotions grows, you will begin to relate to gemstones as healing essences. You will start to wear them more, hold them in your hands more, and have them all around you, so they can amplify the seven colors in the rainbow spectrum that are now being vitalized around your planet. Within the next seven years you will begin to have them in buildings, on the walls, and worn on the body for their balancing properties.

When you become more fully aware of who you are and what your soul ray of intention is, you will be drawn to some colored stones more than others. You will also use color to balance your own energies. For example, you could select the red of a ruby to vitalize the blood, giving a feeling of energy.

You may wonder why there are so many gems and minerals, since you have the rainbow of only seven rays. This is because one color has many levels of intention, so many shades are needed. You have stones that are soft in their hues, and then you have those that are very intense shades. That variety is needed because we do not wish or expect each person to work with the same intensity of commitment to ray purpose.

Density as a quality of gems and minerals relates to the length of time a stone can hold vibrations. As an individual works with the stone, its density becomes personalized and balances with the person's chemistry and energy vibration. The denser, or harder, its composition, the longer the stone will be able to hold the vibration. A diamond, for instance, has the "light" in it, but no real healing power, whereas quartz crystals are living things with the greatest healing qualities of any gem or mineral on Earth.

Now, everything upon your planet was uniquely designed to be here and work with you humans or other living forms. Of course, there are stones on other planets and stars, but the stones here are chemical *compositions from this planet and for this planet.* They were not brought here from some other place.

They are made of the elements of your planet, C-ton, and are carbon-based. Substances require certain chemical elements and then Earth pressure to create them. Because these stones were created of the elements of C-ton alone, they are compatible to *your* energy fields.

Humanity's designation of the term "precious" for gold and silver is interesting to note, for while you have other expensive items such as uranium and plutonium, the two you generally wear and place monetary value upon relate to the first two rays created by God—the Gold and Silver. We notice this with humor and say "thank you" for that. Remember, however, that while gold and silver can work with you as healing metals, they are here in conjunction with the healing stones, not to be superior to them. The actual properties of these metals do not make them as, or any more, precious than a beautiful stone. In fact, metals don't have the great healing properties that a moonstone or an opal or a piece of quartz crystal may have. It is what you do with them that makes them valuable.

Plutonium, uranium, and other "-ium" minerals have not been found in abundance yet, and this is appropriate at this time because they are not being used for peaceful endeavors. With your new electronic devices, however, your planet is becoming smaller and smaller. Those things you call treasures, which are located within the Earth, are becoming more observable. As you use your infra-ray electronic devices to see within, and beyond, the surface of the Earth to identify the minerals and the metals, remember to use your discovery for peaceful purposes only. Let the highly emotional aspect of locating gems, minerals, and metals not be just for avarice and greed but to find materials for health and healing, and spiritual advancement for all life.

There is obviously far more to know about your planet, its contents, and their reasons for being here, than we have said.

Yet, until you resume your responsibilities as caretakers of the Earth, it is not wise to release greater secrets to be misused by technological madmen.

In the coming days you will be amazed at how wise humanity can become! It is hoped that your personalities will receive the greater knowledge without temptation for misuse. Someday, those who would misapply or abuse it will be gone, and the only safe conduits for the greater knowing will be scientists and healers of your world.

Please remember that all of you together are one planetary creation. You, the individual soul, are called forth now to master your experience here as a caretaker and peacemaker. Do this, and your spiritual evolution is assured. This is your hour for demonstration and evaluation.

Chapter VII

Earth and Your Solar System

Now that your astronauts have walked on the Moon and you have seen photographs of other local planets, have you ever wondered why your solar system was created? Or in what order these brother and sister planets came forth? Even as a human family with siblings has order and relationship, do you know which planet is the oldest? Which is the youngest?

Let us give you an understanding about creating a solar system. We began our conceptual design for your system with the choice of circles and near-circles, measured by our special device, the A-bar.

The conceptual design for Cly-ton, your solar system, was based on expressing love for all planets while revering the God force and allowing each planet *free will*. We selected the *family design* concept. Hence, each planet would have a *relationship* to all others. This factor required the use of orbits or avenues of movement. Then we determined that the solar system would have 12 planets or possible places for habitation. (Of those 12, one has been destroyed, and two are coming into your awareness in the future.) Your solar system was based first upon the gravitational pull design *within* each planet and then its relationship *with* the other planets.

103

All twelve planets have gravitational pull, though many with a lesser intensity than C-ton's. Each planet's gravitational pull is adjusted to allow lifeforms on its surface or *interior*, if needed.

There are two aspects of gravitational pull on C-ton. One part forces the material, or planet, together with external pressure. When it reaches a center point going inward, it reverses itself to move outward to a distance of 250 miles beyond the Earth's surface, forming a canopy that allows movement of all lifeforms on the surface.

For your planet the reversal of gravitational pull is aided by its interior heat. Hence, you have interior heat and compression as the matter is held together by the pressure and pull, even as you have the release of energy to allow mobility on the planet. Although the core of your Earth is primarily iron, this heavy weight is not a concern since the gravitational pull is *to* the center.

No planet in your solar system is physically superior to any other, although some are more aesthetic or interesting according to personal preference. Each has a unique quality, typical in families, and each is beloved. Everything is cared about. Thus, after creating your solar system's center point, the Sun, we had a nucleus around which matter or substance could orbit, and we then proceeded to bring forth those planets now more familiar to you in photographs from telescopes and your orbiting devices.

Planets in order of creation
1. Mars
2. Jupiter
3. C-ton
4. Mercury
5. Maldek (destroyed by scientific inhabitants)

6. Uranus
7. Neptune
8. Saturn
9. Venus
10. Will be known
11. Pluto
12. Will be known

According to our predetermined plan, we selected the placement of the 12 planets. Our determination for placement of planets is based on a mathematical calculation of movement, weight, and substance. We create one planet, review, and then place another dense form in relationship to the prior one and those to follow.

Notice in your list above that the planet known to us as Maldek no longer exists. Those godless scientists blew it up with hydrogen, causing great damage to other life besides accomplishing their own planetary suicide. But no other planet in your system will be allowed to do the same. That is why we are here—to help you use free will and avoid catastrophe.

Maldek was formerly in position between Jupiter and Saturn. Saturn was further out, but was drawn closer to Jupiter, or closer *into* the orbit of Maldek, when Maldek exploded. The subsequent magnetic pull that resulted from the vacancy did not push Saturn out. Rather, due to its light weight, Saturn was drawn toward the Sun, collected Maldek's debris around it in a magnetic pattern, and established a new orbit—all with our help.

The two other planets presently unknown to you await your "discovery." One is between Mars and Jupiter; one is located beyond Pluto. Both planets are small by your measurements—approximately the size of Mars.

Some information about your solar system has already been released by the galactic and intergalactic forces, other Earth dwellers who channel, and by space entities who have landed here to contact your planet directly. However, we shall give a simple picture ourselves so you can have a basic overview of who's who in your solar system.

DESCRIPTION OF THE PLANETS

PLUTO

Pluto is presently your furthest known planet from the Sun, and its lifeforms are not designated to filter much information to your planet just now. Those inhabitants are smaller, shorter, and wider in size than earthlings. They have a flatter head that does not completely rise above the torso or body.

Their intelligence level is lower than the average intelligence on Earth, and their population numbers about 4.2 million. They are also in a lower dimension and are not discernible by humans. Why? The lifeforms on other planets or star clusters are not of the same substance as you. They are of a physical density that is not *carbon-based*. Therefore, since your existence is related to your planet and all of the elements that relate to it, you cannot see beings of another substance.

Your vision, your senses, your feelings—everything relates to *your* environment—so you are not able to have stellar vision. You are using only a small percentage of your brain. Later, the factor of vision that relates to seeing matter, molecules, or atomic structure—things seemingly different from your human composition—may develop somewhat.

URANUS

Life on Uranus is represented by animal lifeforms only. As perceived by your eyes, some would look like those domestic animals called cows, horses, goats, sheep, cats, dogs, and so on. Their spiritual dimension of 3.4 is slightly lower than your 3.6. They also are invisible to your sight. However, they may contact humans in the dream state to bring messages regarding your planet and to make you less afraid of different shaped lifeforms. About 2.6 million Uranians exist.

VENUS
Venus is the only other planet with a lifeform anywhere near to what you know as human. Venusians are less dense in body than you but have active intelligence and a caring disposition, though not to the level of love possible on Earth. There are now a few souls here from Venus as "walk-ins" to assist during the Time of Awakening.

SATURN
Saturn's life energies are highly evolved with a 3.7 dimension. They are intellectual and caring, but they do not express the same heartfelt emotion that humans of Earth can epitomize. Population would be about 10 million.

Although Saturnians have a caring aspect which is almost totally balanced with their intellect, it is not emotional love. Nonetheless, because of their concern, they do the "policing" of the solar system and are its official governmental/tribunal site. Technologically astute, these beings would assist humanity toward peaceful application of many useful inventions. Although Saturn holds the governing body for the welfare of the entire solar system, your home territory regrettably has no representative on it due to your present unconsciousness. A caring space being called Monka has been appointed to represent your planet's interests, however.

Because Saturnians are so intelligent, they can project themselves through space to investigate other places within the

107

solar system and are ideally suited to the responsibility of watching over the solar system. Although they can travel using thought forms, they primarily use intergalactic vehicles for prolonged visits to other planets in the solar system, including Earth. Their physical appearance is invisible to you and has only a little physical density to its vertical form. Their arms are infrequently used and generally out of sight. Unlike you, they have no feet or legs.

After the insane destruction of the planet Maldek, the Saturnians had to establish protective rings to guard themselves from the exploding debris. With our aid a reversed gravitational force field was put in place to stop this debris from smashing into the planet. This force field caught the various materials and particles to prevent penetration beyond a certain point, and that debris is still held in orbit by this force field and the motion of the moving matter. A change in this situation is not presently anticipated since any removal might affect your entire solar system.

Each planet can protect itself, but it must have the consciousness and technological wisdom to do so. Although the pockmarked places now visible on Mars and the Moon had nothing to do with Maldek, there is an asteroid belt due to Maldek's demise.

JUPITER

Jupiter is another highly evolved planet with lifeforms closely matching the intelligence of Saturnians. It is larger in size but is sparingly populated. The population is in the interior of the planet and inside its Titan moon. Their intelligence is technically oriented with some caring aspect. They are about six feet tall, narrow in appearance, and have an unusual *horizontal* energy flow within their body form.

108

Jupiter, Saturn, and Venus have intergalactic space vehicles, and they frequently visit among themselves and nearby regions. They only make contact with Earth intermittently. We are endeavoring to include more knowledge about them by channeling information so that your stories, your songs, and your awareness will confirm that other lifeforms exist beyond this planet.

Your scientists seek other lifeforms "out there", yet you tend to deny their existence when they visit Earth. You desire to dominate other lifeforms which makes you dangerous! Although space brothers and sisters do exist, you still have not reached a point where that reality and communication are accepted by you.

NEPTUNE
Neptune is not designated to have fully developed life energies at this time, contrary to what we hear some people saying.

MERCURY
Mercury's energies are different. Mercury is a place where some lifeforms from Earth and other planets go for consultation and lifetime reviews before returning to Earth or their former homes. Mercury's semi-permanent population is small, only 100,000. The energies are four to five feet tall. They are whitish with a red hue or tint. Their countenance is light or translucent. They would be on a spiritual dimensionality of six, because they are there as teachers.

MARS
Mars' surface is not inhabited at this time, though a few inhabitants remain underground. The greater population has moved elsewhere because it used up its water and the inhabitants were forced to depart or die. Some came to Earth from

that once thriving planet, but primarily they have gone to other places within the universe.

They actually look like the little spacemen your filmmakers and cartoonists portray and that have been seen here. But they are light brown, not green, in color. Although they now come from a variety of other places, they resemble each other because they *first* came from Mars and migrated elsewhere. Now they are seeking your planet primarily for its water and to learn how you retain your water.

Transportation of water back to Mars is possible since water can be changed into vapors and different molecular consistencies. They are endeavoring to make water from plant precipitation, as well. They may be here, also, to determine the possibility of their lifeforms living upon this planet (by agreement).

Martians are on a dimension of 3.3, which means they are still within the third dimension but are making progress toward a higher level. They contact the Earth frequently but are not highly intellectual or communicative. A large percentage of visible spaceships are Martian, although you are being contacted from many different places.

It is interesting that your space photos of Mars show a giant pyramid left there because its substance would not destruct or evaporate, as did the water. One of the vital things about your planet is its water. Life on this planet will not exist without water, a fact not to be taken lightly. Water is your very life, as the Martians found out.

Besides visits and contacts from your neighboring planets, many intergalactic travel and communication sources are coming to Earth now, and these visits will intensify from 1988 on. In fact, there will be a total review of all intergalactic communications with this planet—a total review of everything about your planet—after the two-year period ending November, 1988. We will keep you informed about all this, of course.

Although some of the "UFO's" that visit you contain weapons, they are not intended to harm you. In fact, most of them are here with definite instructions to aid you. Some of them wish to get information, as well as give it, and they are monitoring information about your minerals. Others are here to give medical information and to bring harmony to your planet.

Now, about the Moon. It is not really a planet. It is designated as a *reflective device* to give nighttime illumination to Earth to reduce fear and to remind you of the Silver Ray energy, and the continuance of life. The Moon reminds you that day and night are but two parts of the one creation. You and each planet in your solar system have three to five reflective moons or light bodies to provide sufficient nightlight, although you do not label them as such. Two very intense stars are Earth's other moons and will be so noted by your astronomers eventually.

The Moon also works with the gravitational pull of your planet to keep your body upon the Earth. As you learn to live in harmony with this pull you will be able to grow more abundant crops, learn about physical health, and work concurrently with your seasons. Your Moon cycles can help you live in harmony with the planet itself. Since the Moon's force is there even when the Earth is cloud-covered, your computers can analyze these pulls to assist modification of human activities for rhythm compatibility.

The Moon is a relay station with only transient life. When your astronauts went to the Moon and on other missions, they returned with the telepathic awareness that lifeforms exist beyond the Earth. A few of them actually saw beings different than humans, a fact that your governments have refused to believe or have withheld and denied.

111

The Moon has many uses. It is a relay station where an energy can come from a distant place and rest. Other souls go there following an Earth death, or transition, and have a spiritual review or shortterm evaluation to see if they wish to return to Earth. Because it is closely related to the lower astral levels and energies, there is life on the Moon at the etheric level but not on the physical plane. Its dimension rating varies according to what is occurring and which lifeforms are involved. Many beings use it because of its proximity to the Earth.

Regarding the Sun, it was created to radiate heat, or *energy*, to your solar system. It is a source of rejuvenation to the planets, and it also contains some lifeforms. These are high-level intelligent beings not permanently situated there. The primary concern or purpose of the Sun in your solar system is to monitor physical life harmony and progress. Information about the physical existence and relationship of all lifeforms is filtered through this area.

The Sun surveys your space development and explorations beyond the Earth and also the relationship of Venusian travel within the rest of the solar system. The Sun monitors all this activity as well as giving heat, or what is called nourishment, through the radiance of its energy. It has some spiritual advisors residing within it, but they are not in charge of the spiritual aspects of the solar system. Each planet is to sustain its own spiritual life. Nonetheless, because your non-caring spiritual attitudes endanger other lifeforms at *physical* levels, you represent a threat to life's design and purpose. This threat is what brings us forth.

Although Earth is on the far edge of the 12th Universe, it is a place of interest, a place of beauty. Because many of the 11 million souls who were the caretakers here originally came from elsewhere, the intergalactic spaceships, which travel on frequencies, meridians, or avenues, occasionally come to Earth.

Sometimes they make contact, sometimes not; sometimes they make their ships visible, sometimes not. To become visible to earthlings creates a danger or hazard for space travelers, but this is their choice. They may either survey or land and make contact, as they wish. They usually just gather their information, lift off, and go back to a chosen course of travel.

Within this universe and your solar system, intergalactic travel actually occurs, just as you travel on your planet from one city to another or from one nation to another. This stellar travel is a reality in dimensions and frequencies that are not perceived by your human eye. Perhaps there are times when you look out from the corner of your eye and can perceive beings from other dimensions, but most humans are too fearful to bear this vision.

Intergalactic or stellar travel is a term we use to denote a more sophisticated or developed mode of travel than you have. *There are no present restrictions on peaceful travel from the Milky Way galaxy to your solar system.* Please ponder this information well.

EARTH

Before we conclude our discussion of your solar system, let us briefly mention Earth, for you know very little about it even as you reside there this moment. Did you know that Earth is spiritually the darkest of the nine planets, having experienced turmoil and war for eons? Did you know that although most of your lifeforms live on the planet's surface, a few beings live *inside* the center of the Earth? Little information should be made public about them at this time because it could create confusion and distort the program we are focusing to humanity's surface dwellers. But they are there.

Suffice to say, those living underground are remnants from ancient civilizations such as Atlantis and Lemuria who have information that could aid the *surface humans*. If their emergence to the surface and interrelation with the surface people wouldn't cause worship or misuse of power, the information disclosures they bring would be harmless and could help raise human intelligence. It would be necessary for them to merge into *modern* time, however, for the past is gone, and you are *not* to dwell upon it. Soul-mastery and peace occur only in the present moment!

If a great rush of communication and inner-earth contact should begin, the results could be negative for humanity. Consequently, this contact must be handled carefully to avoid interrupting your evolutionary progress, as well as that of the inner beings. You must not get involved with their past and they somehow have to give up their prior experiences and come into your present world.

Earth has a great potential for a harmonious relationship with its solar and extraterrestial family. The excitement of relating to cousins, if you would like to use that term, could bring great joy and learning. These beings who care and could help you move quickly to a higher status are nearby. Your medical knowledge could be rapidly increased. The development of the planet itself—irrigation, water purification, healing of the land, and aiding the desert areas to bloom more quickly—could occur. Your populations wouldn't have to be jammed up in a few large areas; you could again populate the entire planet. You could also travel to other planets and develop happy relationships, just as you now travel to another nation and come back with pleasant memories.

Yes, you could experience great harmony within your planet which would be enjoyable for you and a gift to the solar system's life, as well. But you must first eliminate the destructive aspects of your technology to win this goal. Wanting to control and kill fellow creations is not a natural, spiritual inclination! Surely you know this. Yet you allow some war-loving beings to spoil your potential glory as a jewel of the universe. It is urgent and absolutely necessary that you take a personal stand on this issue.

As we conclude this information about your 12th solar system, I will mention two other, now unseen, planets that will eventually be revealed to Earth: Vetar and Natar.

VETAR AND NATAR
Vetar has lifeforms on it. Natar, the smaller, does not. Vetar has the probability of coming into viewing about 1992 in your time and Natar between about 1998 and 2010 A.D., *but these dates are only approximate.* One or both of these planets could be used for educational purposes in the event Earth souls do not choose a "yes" to God and "yes" to peaceful behavior. We are preparing the solar system environment for whatever will come, unbelievable as this may seem to you! All necessary physical conditions will be in alignment and readiness as humanity travels its spiritual journey through the Time of Awakening.

We hear conversation about a planet called Vulcan, but there is no planet by that name scheduled to appear in *your* solar system. Perhaps one of the above planets has been misinterpreted or given a different name?

Finally, a word concerning the comets that come and go in your solar system. Comets are created matter that we use for two purposes: one, to observe the movement of created matter within a solar system, galaxy, or universe; and two, to demonstrate that life exists beyond your Earth plane, and you have no power over it. A comet's orbit also allows collection of data for storage and retrieval by other forces, primarily those of Saturn or Jupiter. Your scientists say comets are made of ice, as perceived by their instruments. Yes, comets may contain ice at some stage, but a comet is not always solid when it travels. As it transforms from a gaseous state to a more solid form such as ice, it absorbs and retains many types of information that can be monitored and inspected by those who know its composition and purpose. Have you ever looked at a piece of ice and noticed that it contains many particles?

You of Earth have much to learn, and that process is being accelerated by the vibratory increase we have instituted. At the same time, and I offer this thought kindly, the more you learn the more you will need to learn if you are to save the planet. You must understand the greatest truth of all: learning never ends! But without reverence for God, learning brings only tragedy.

You will never be able to see the edge or length of a universe. Neither will you be able to count all of the created matter within it. So the more you learn, the more you will have to learn. For you it is truly a never ending quest, but you will delight in the challenge.

If you commit to positive cosmic intention and correct usage of universal law, we will deny you nothing. But you must respect all life on your planet and beyond because other dimensions would suffer if you were to damage physical life with hydrogen and nuclear explosions. For example, Maldek's explosion created an asteroid belt and threw solid rock mass out into space, affecting some faraway stars as well as neighboring galactic planets. Without our assistance in Saturn's dangerous situation, your own solar system could have been seriously harmed.

One of the properties of hydrogen is that although its damage is not always immediately discernible, it can continue to react in a chain reaction. It could conceivably go through a space meridian and harm all it contacted within that specified area. Consequently, following the hydrogen destruction of

116

Maldek, a cosmic charter was made to prohibit such an event from ever happening again. All life—and you—is bound by that agreement forever.

Suffice to say, do *not* harm space or your own homeland. Instead, seek peace and harmony in all you do. This is the way of growth and service we request. Please treat others in the fashion suggested in your holy books, and bring no harm to another.

It is essential that you comprehend and practice universal law. Your universe and solar system are static in one way, but ever changing in another. *Static* means that the stars and planets each have assigned orbits where they have been placed by us and where they are to remain. So the law is: remain where assigned! Changing of established physical orbits is not allowed due to the chaos and destruction this would cause other cosmic neighbors.

Neither may any energy meridians or avenues in space be changed, damaged or abused, since they are used by galactic beings for a myriad of transportation purposes. What you call UFO's require these particularized energy points for terrestial, dimensional, galactic, and intergalactic travel. Like the highways and roads of your planet, they are to be kept open and repaired at all times. These are busy, busy places.

There in space, amidst the teeming activities of life beyond your imagination, beings at varying levels of wisdom live out their roles in an eternal drama of cosmic proportions.

High above you, twinkling in the nighttime sky, trillions of adventures are played out in physical and spiritual worlds beyond your present comprehension. Unseen and unknown as they may be, your planet could truly cause disruption and even disaster to their worlds. Kindly care for these unseen ones. You are family of the One Parent through the first two born of God. Never forget this. Then be concerned for your own

117

planet and all life upon it. In addition, be considerate of all that lies beyond Earth's small boundary.

Learn self-control and discipline among yourselves, practice the stewardship that caretaking requires, and you can gain personal and planetary growth.

Your opportunity is *now*. We stand ready to aid all who seek advancement through caring and compassion, or love and wisdom.

May peace reign upon the most beautiful creation in your universe. Let it occur because of *your* soul intention and personal actions!

ILLUSTRATIONS

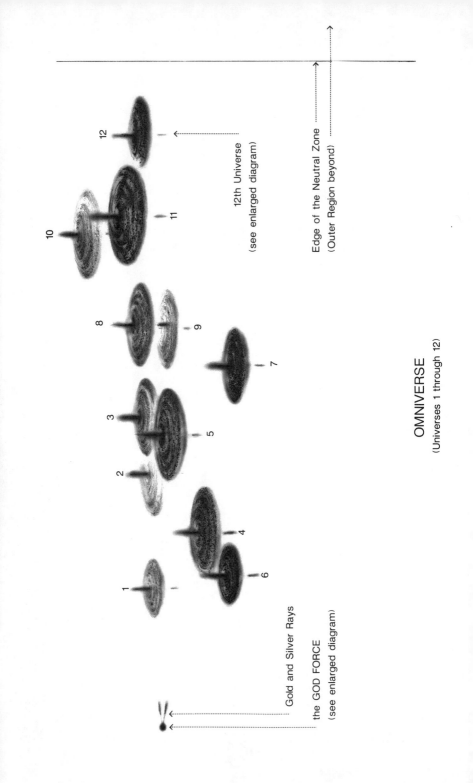

OMNIVERSE
(Universes 1 through 12)

12th Universe
(see enlarged diagram)

Edge of the Neutral Zone
(Outer Region beyond)

Gold and Silver Rays

the GOD FORCE
(see enlarged diagram)

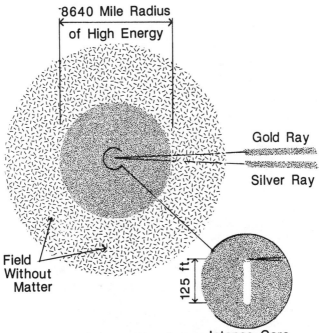

8640 Mile Radius of High Energy

Gold Ray

Silver Ray

Field Without Matter

125 ft.

Intense Core

THE GOD FORCE
The GOD Area is Small in Cosmic Creation
IT is the Beginning
THE SOURCE

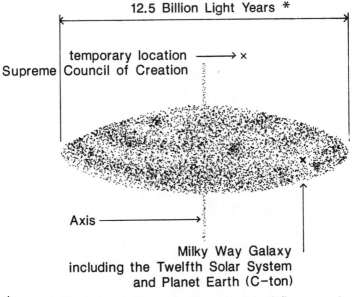

12.5 Billion Light Years *

temporary location ⟶ ×

Supreme Council of Creation

Axis ⟶

Milky Way Galaxy
including the Twelfth Solar System
and Planet Earth (C–ton)

*The use of existing systems of measurement to define space is
inadequate. The vastness of the Omniverse cannot be
understood until the human species discovers hyperspace.

THE TWELFTH UNIVERSE

Chapter VIII

The Omniverse and You

Just as one universe is defined as being many creations united into a meaningful structure or form, so the Omniverse is that gigantic combination that brings all of existence into a unified relationship. It is the sum total of physical and spiritual creation.

Although you do not perceive them now, your own universe contains multitudes of lifeforms and physical creations united for a cause called compatibility. Even if you cannot grasp the details of something as large as the Omniverse, we ask you to try for a *feeling* of this unending development and expansion. Even if it boggles your intellect's attempts to define it within present earthly limitation and perception, let your soul recognize and claim cosmic identity.

This matrix of ever expanding creation is your greater homeland, even if you can only sense or imagine portions of it. As each holy light universe was birthed with a vast variety of physical and spiritual lifeforms, we gained knowledge for future experimentation and support. Thus, your 12th Universe contains more variety than all that has gone before, and you of Earth are the benefactors.

You are a link in a chain of starlight creations with unceasing expansion. What the Great Rays do or observe on your

119

planet will assist other lifeforms, whether already in existence or awaiting the miracle of birth. Appreciate what has been given; appreciate what is yours now. In so doing your future relationship to creation is assured at the highest possible level. Claim your ancient heritage by solving your present challenge on Earth. Preserve life, for it has such cosmic origins you would weep with your soul's remembrance of its glorious, magnificent procession.

There are many creations in the Omniverse with its 24 spiritual levels or dimensions and the ten levels of physical body density, and we are attempting to clarify your role in a three dimensional world that has both the spiritual and physical levels. Since your planet has the rare gift of free will, we hope this clarification will aid you in choosing wisely what that role is to be.

Beyond your present sight are two types of life, then: that of the brothers and sisters of the physical worlds and that of invisible beings from etheric or high spiritual realms. Both of these groups have influenced C-ton at different times since its beginning. However, the first caretakers to your planet were from a high *physical* density level of eight, and it is to this level we would have you return from your present five to six range as soon as possible.

Then accept that long ago, before your planet could have had caretakers, there either had to be soul life that would volunteer to go there or else new souls would have to be created. Since you are on Earth, you must belong to one of these groups; you must be one of its caretakers. We have, therefore, included a picture of the God force and Great Rays, and of the Omniverse with its twelve universes, so you can see your own location in the general design of things. I also will describe the levels of our universal "team" so you may understand in greater depth "who's who" in the higher regions of the Omniverse. Thus, when channeled information is released, you will have a better sense of our levels and can ask beings to identify their level of spiritual consciousness and physical body density to you. This should give you greater confidence and assurance when meeting so-called entities or invisible energies through channeling. Now look at the illustration of the God force. At its most intense core it is level 24, and in the protective energized area around the God force core itself, it is level 23. Not even we Rays can enter these two levels! Then notice how God produced the two first-born creations, or Rays, for this is where life's creative process originated. We are level 22, and from us all physical matter, lifeforms, and light forms emanated. Get a sense of that beginning so we can clarify how all-encompassing the Omniverse is and how it operates. From God came the Gold and Silver Rays. From the Rays the creation of physical matter and life began. Then came life for souls and all living things, and a team of helpers to run the Omniverse and its many activities.

For example, have you ever heard of the 24 ancient ones, or the Elohim, who we created after the very first physical universe to observe, record, and store historical events of all universes? Their archives contain information about the physical matter worlds and the energy lifeforms who inhabit them. Perhaps one day we will release some of this information for your further education.

The ancient Elohim are rays about 20 feet high who reside in a circle around the outer rim of the God force energy at spiritual dimension, or level, 22, a system of numbering downward in scale from us to you. (You are presently within level, or dimension, three.)

The Elohim themselves do not create energy lifeforms or physical matter, but they keep the documents describing these

121

events in the sacred chambers that are under their guardianship.

All cosmic data about matter and lifeforms is forwarded to the Elohim where they record it. Yet at the same time it goes *beyond* them to the God force, and that One's response is then filtered back for recording also. In this communication loop the Elohim are responsible for receipt and retrieval of all knowledge.

Please try to comprehend that all information, all vibrations, and all frequencies that relate to God and the level 22 spiritual realm are happening simultaneously. That which relates to the Silver Ray, the Gold Ray, the Elohim, and the God force occurs concurrently. Perhaps you can understand this idea by recalling that thought is an energy frequency, like your voice, which creates sound waves. You have experienced, also, a radio or television broadcast with many receptive units—perhaps 5 million—tuned to one station at the same time. They may need relay units, but primarily it is one station beaming information out, or broadcasting, to many awaiting receivers. The different beings that receive the information at the same time use it differently.

That which is the God force takes it all in and communicates back to the Rays through different impulses. The Rays filter it through different channels and decide what needs immediate attention. Because we can "read" the energy that comes from each universe out of what we call its top axis—an energy sensor, port, or input area—any extreme negativity, such as Earth's, brings instant notice. It is through these axis areas that we monitor and respond to energy levels. We can discern the output and respond by visitation or by sending our ray energies through that port.

We—and the God force—have received many distress signals forwarded up from the highest cosmic levels; some come from the great intergalactic councils and continue right on down to your solar tribunals, and Earth's light workers, as well.

From these many pleas and cosmic communications, plus our own evaluation, we have defined your status as so critical that we Rays, ourselves, have descended in vibration to assist your reclamation. This is a joyful moment for Earth, but it has also created intense problems in communication with humanity. For few Earth beings are open to the type of information we bring. Thus, what is called "channeling" has become our major tool, and you are being beamed constant helpful information through those who are willing, receptive communicators. Some may be personal messages, but important ones are to be written down and shared.

We have chosen this direct communication because of the *emergency* nature of your situation. The changes we bring require immense cooperation and understanding among your teachers on levels four, five, six, and seven. Why? Because all of the spiritual teaching realms you are in contact with are having to revamp and update their educational programs in terms of these rapid decisions and movements on our part. Past information is obsolete. Then appreciate your usual spiritual guides and teachers, and know how pressed they are by our unprecedented intervention to instantaneously adapt to the level of information we bring. Ordinary information or non-critical decisions would usually flow down from level 22 and then be lowered further still to the dimensions involved. In your third dimension this takes "time."

Therefore, you may be experiencing some confusion on Earth until the massive communication effort we have undertaken becomes better coordinated and more cohesive. Again we are surprised by your naive belief that at a single decision each created being—from both physical and spiritual levels—should perfectly understand and comply with our plan to help you. Life is beautiful in the higher regions, but it is not yet perfected outside of God. If you can grasp this fact, and accept it without resistance, we will all be able to work together for the benefit of your planet and the preservation of life everywhere.

If you ask, then, why there is so much confusion regarding the information being received on Earth today from spiritual realms, the answer is simple. Communication has to descend in vibrational sequence to your universe, then down to your galaxy, and finally to your level three. There are many steps in that gigantic ladder between us! As I, the Silver Ray, send information to all top-level beings, there is the hope that each being in charge of communicating the information to the next level below does this accurately so that eventually, when it gets to the one needing to implement it, it is still the same message!

You have the same problem of communication on Earth. Unless you can write or speak *directly* to the individual involved, you never know with 100 percent accuracy what has transpired. Even then perfection is illusive. The majority of formerly useful teaching material and esoteric information is now out of date and must be reviewed. *Past* documents may be invalid for specific current events. If you want to know today's weather, which report do you prefer to listen to—last year's or the most current? As mentioned, that is one reason we have opened up direct contact through "channels" on your planet. If they are fairly pure receivers, it is the quickest, most reliable method of current communication possible. Channels can be cosmic telephones to a world asleep in its own self-perpetuating ignorance.

It is this same prophetic gift that brought forth information about nearly every major world religion, is that not so? But more will be said about channeling later on.

Now let us return to our discussion about the level 22 realm and coordination of all Omniverse matters. Since, as a human being, you are a friendly creature who likes having a family or companionship, perhaps you can understand why the Gold and Silver Rays would create other lifeforms and energies? After birthing the 24 Elohim, the Silver Ray, apart from the Gold, created eleven offspring. The first-born was called Silver Ray "minor" and was very powerful. (This one is now called the Rebel Ray or the dark ray.) Of the other ten subrays, three are invisible to your eyes, but seven are seen by Earth dwellers as the rainbow.

SUBRAYS

A subray is an ancient offspring from the Silver Ray's energy that has a single color, such as green, and one single quality or intention, such as healing, as its focus. Seven of these are visible to you on Earth, beginning with red, orange, yellow, green, blue, indigo, and purple. This is called your rainbow spectrum.

Each of these subrays measures a half-mile by a quarter-mile in size. Each is flat and horizontal so it can travel through space easily in any direction. Like its parent, a subray's movement is unlimited. The aliveness of a subray's molecular content is so closely knit that if you were to see the energy you would think it solid, though it is not.

As mentioned, each separate ray has within it *one* distinctive quality or frequency, which can be amplified or modified to accomplish its primary service. Yet the subray itself is a force without intellect or personality. It moves into the different universes, as needed, under the guidance of super-beings called "masters." There is one master for each color subray. Thus, here on Earth, Hilarion is master of the Green Ray's energy and utilizes it to express the multi-leveled quality of healing that is contained in its electromagnetic nature.

This chart may be helpful in clarifying the colors and the

masters. The chapter on your ray of intention has already explained the quality of each ray.

Ray Color	Master
Red, scarlet or ruby	Archangel Gabriel
Orange	Makeon
Yellow	Alaeon
Green	Hilarion (Earth soul)
Blue	Archangel Michael
Indigo	A great being soon to come
Violet or purple	St. Germain (Earth soul)

On your planet at this time you have Lords of Light from the angelic realms and two Earth souls as your ray masters or directors.

St. Germain and Hilarion are not Lords of Light but are souls who have, through various Earth incarnations, attained a high degree of illumination and demonstrated many loving actions. Because they have risen by virtue of devotion and service, you call them "ascended" masters. Ascended means proceeding upward *from* the Earth plane *to* a higher spiritual level. Please do not confuse an "ascended" master with a master of the ray. There are many ascended masters, but only two of them have been designated for this rare responsibility with the rays.

Then how is a "master" of a ray defined, you may ask. It is a title of authority. Master carries less authority than Lord of Light, but a Lord of Light may use his power(s) in a lesser capacity to accomplish certain purposes when there is no other being available to handle the situation.

A Lord of Light is one who has been selected from the angelic realms because of excellent service in heavenly domains and who descends into the Earth plane for service. These have never been incarnated in a physical body.

Perhaps it will be more clear to say a master is a director or user of the ray, nominated either from Earth's spiritual family or the Lords of Light. The names of Gabriel and Michael, who are Lords of Light, also carry your special Earth terminology of Archangel, but we in our realm do not use this description. Your term Archangel derives from what was once described to the Earth eons ago as Arch-being. Not understanding what a being was, you substituted angel and have since called the Arch-being, or very powerful one, Archangel.

We use the term Lords of Light, or the subtitle: Illuminator. We shall speak more of this shortly.

A subray is used by its master to focus that color's quality to a person, place, or thing that needs it. Thus, the Purple Ray of peace is currently being implemented by St. Germain to change the Earth's vibration through intensification of the peace aspect. The Purple Ray can be beamed around the entire globe or finely tuned to an organization, a project, a group, or even a person for certain periods of time. You may think of it as shining a bright light or turning up the color frequency in a designated area.

All members of the Supreme Council or the Silver Ray can also control a ray's amplification and direction.

LORDS OF LIGHT

After creating the subrays, the Silver Ray needed a large work force to assist in the further expansion of the universes and, with the Gold Ray's assent, brought forth one million little energies or rays, only four feet long and one-half foot wide. These energies were first used throughout space as scouts, messengers, and fast-moving communicators.

From these small, lesser assistants in creation, much was learned about size and movement, and your spiritual books are filled with tales of their comings and goings. You call them angels.

Approximately one hundred of these small assistants were selected or promoted because of excellent service, and their size was increased to twenty feet in height. These are the Lords of Light who have great intelligence, memory, and spiritual intention. These Illuminators radiate their light in service to that which has been created. Or more simply put, they are God-like in their nature or essence. On our spiritual dimension scale they place somewhere between levels 12 and 18. At this time, all of the Lords of Light are working to refine the life that has already been created, and two of them—Gabriel and Michael—are acting as masters of the subrays for C-ton.

Although created by the Silver Ray, it is the Gold Ray who gave the Lords of Light and other angelic creations forcefulness, endurance, and illumination, so if you see these angelic forms, you usually see them with the Gold Ray's illumination as well as with some silvery light. Thus, that which is perceived in any vision of great angels may have this combination of gold and silver radiance.

Please note: A Lord of Light is different than the great Christ Light energy of the Gold Ray.

SUPREME COUNCIL OF CREATION

There is also a special group of beings who were created during the third universe to assist in designing new lifeforms and other important work done under the Silver Ray's aegis. They are presently here to assist Earth, along with many other high-level beings. These eight are collectively called the Supreme Council of Creation. Please note in the illustration section their current but temporary vantage point near your 12th Universe's axis.

Each of these beings has a particular personal specialty or responsibility, but all have general duties as well. These include overseeing and evaluating lifeforms, activities, and circumstances in any quadrant or area of the Omniverse that may need modification, enhancement, or attention. In Earth terms they would be high administrators in function. Nonetheless, they are called to alert in situations such as your Earth emergency and, along with the Lords of Light and the Great Rays, have come to change your present dilemma.

An example of a Supreme Council member's individual expertise is Serton (Sir-tawn), who is in charge of bringing scientific information and development to a state of pure intention.

This description has briefly summarized the support team, created by the Silver Ray, to carry out the many tasks related to the creation and nurturance of life. Notice that the Gold Ray has focused primarily on one single purpose and has only one Lord of Light on his ray. This one is called Sananda, who is the great teacher representative to the many universes. While thousands of other beings are allowed to use the Gold Ray for teaching purposes, they teach only at the site where the ray has penetrated or focused, such as Earth where many great ones have used the Christ Light or Christ Consciousness to instruct the populace about God.

The Gold Ray has been father to them all, but because the one called Jesus has been more *lovingly* dedicated to humanity for the past 2,000 years, he has earned the title of World Teacher for Earth and coordinates your present awakening program.

It is a miracle, indeed, that he, the entire hierarchy of the Omniverse, and 5 million volunteers should attend your tiny planet and call humanity forward to its hour of fruition.

You may be wondering what these beings do when they are not helping Earth and I tell you, truly, we are all *busy*. That is why we cannot stay long, and you of Earth must assume your own responsibilities. We have many tasks of nurturance elsewhere. Even on your Earth you hopefully disband the majority of your armies when there is no war.

Now long ago in the beginning, the Silver and Gold Ray energies simply experimented, and there was no single purpose or grand design in creation. We just followed the *impulse* of creativity in us and experimented with different aspects of our God-impregnated energies. We had to learn our powers by doing. Just as you, on a human level, reach a point where you cannot think of anything new, or cannot grasp how to cope with a novel situation, but then expand your awareness and proceed, so did we. As we willingly progressed into new experimentations, we expressed the fuller potential of God's nature in us. Thus, all universes are unique in some way and have a particular focus of intent, although they might build on things learned in previous expressions. This is true in dense physical matter worlds and for all lifeforms, soul and soulless.

CONSTRUCTION OF THE UNIVERSE

The actual "construction" of a universe may be of interest to you. It is begun by a mathematical selection of the center point, or axis, to be used for the universe. Using a "vertical" energy not presently known to you, we create an axis of highly concentrated, intensified energy from which the rest of the universe radiates out horizontally as it is created. In other words, we start with a funnel-type focal point and create outward from that axis or port.

You have something similar in the "cotton candy" you buy at amusement parks. There is a vertical paper pole and then the rapid whirling of sugar particles which adhere together around its base and give it substance.

We, of course, use our axis to sense, monitor, or input energy for support of life, and since no two universes are identical (see New Teachings for an Awakening Humanity), we have unique challenges in each of the twelve universes.

After starting the third universe, we decided to specialize, and the Silver Ray became the (feminine) creator for the remaining universes. This *creation by experimentation* continued unabated, and by the 12th Universe the novel concept of free will and variety were instituted.

It is the uniqueness of this 12th Universe experiment—free will—that has already caused you a painful experience from which we wish to extricate you. So let us be frank and state things as they are.

You are truly the prodigal sons and daughters awaiting your estate. Whether you remember or not, you were a created lifeform of high vibration. Your soul has already been brought forth and sparked with God's life. In this there is no choice. Your only choice is *how* that energy will be spent or lived. In that decision you have enormous power.

By explaining the physical dimension levels in simple terms, with a chart to aid your understanding, you will see that you have lost several steps of the vibratory nature you once had. We now offer you the chance to gain them back again, if you wish, and return to the light.

Please look at the Density Scale of Physical Body Lifeforms a moment and notice that in your universe the highest vibratory rating is ten. If you were presently a ten rating, you would not have the flesh and blood body that you wear now but would be an eternal beam, or ray, of light, about seven feet tall, capable of great intelligence. You would possess a molecular structure that could penetrate denser materials to monitor, relate, and explore the physical worlds of which you are now temporarily a part. You would glow and gleam very brightly but would be invisible to the lower dimensions, even as we are invisible to you.

Density Scale of Physical Body Lifeforms in the 12th Universe

10	lightest physical body vibrations in your *universe*; not flesh and blood
9	....
8	present density level for beings in your *solar system*, from Saturn and Venus; not flesh and blood, your *former* rating
7	....
6	....

==

Needs very dense physical forms

5	C-ton or Earth at present between 5 and 6; flesh and blood
4	other dense physical forms
3	„ „ „ „
2	„ „ „ „
1	densest or heaviest physical form

Vibrations go *up* in frequency

Look next at level eight, and notice that it is a very high achievement for those in your solar system. Can you sense that once you were at such a level? That you did not have a dense "flesh and blood" body but lived in more of a light form body? Is it possible that you used space vehicles in the solar system and beyond? Were you really able to soar along the great meridians of the galaxy and yet responsibly care for your home planet and the solar system, as well?

Finally, look at scale five and up one notch to six. Humanity presently hovers between the density of the lower half of the scale, yet also bridges back into the higher levels from whence it came.

These physical body density levels are, in fact, part of the many mansions of your physical universe. Then, of course, there are the forms *beyond* the physical. Let us establish three definitions that will help you understand your own physical level and the levels who may contact you from invisible realms.

Physical Body

Since a low physical density means that a body is, as you say, "flesh and blood," then it cannot permanently abandon the particular environment in which it dwells unless it can substitute the life-giving energies elsewhere or carry them along in some portable fashion. Physical bodies on your planet need physical light to grow and be nurtured. For this purpose you have both the Sun's and the Moon's light. Where would you, the planet, and all of life be without both of them? Yes, your physical essence relates to physical light. Is not one of your childhood fears related to darkness? By contrast, a being from Saturn or Jupiter might have vastly different light needs.

Lifeform

Oftentimes our realm uses the term "lifeform" very loosely to include *anything* that contains an essence of life as a physical creation—plants, animals, and things you have never even dreamed of—not just your human bodies. You think of life in a very restrictive sense, but to us it is all-encompassing. We hope that this is not too confusing.

Light form

An essence of energy or light with only a little molecular density is evident beginning with level six. Many of what you call angels and the very high spiritual ones beyond level twelve have no molecular density. However, these light forms have an outline or perimeter to contain their high intensity vibrations. They became a self-perpetuating radiance that continually recharges itself and is eternal.

Now these various *physical* body forms, *life*forms, and *light* forms populate your universe in galactic profusion on a vast array of stars, star clusters, planets, and so on. Therefore, the Omniverse is an accumulation of physical/material objects—mineral, animal, and plant experiments and souls evolving into higher levels of consciousness. It is an ever-changing, ever-progressing chain of events called experience.

Like some immense orbiting mineral collection—in all colors, sizes, and purposes—some of these physical objects and creative expressions become available for habitation and life seeding. Then begins an endless journey of souls to explore, settle, and develop these places through expanded use of their own creative efforts under cosmic guidelines.

There are more planets, stars, and heavenly bodies than your planet has trees. More souls than all the animals of your flocks! More adventure and excitement than sunbeams on a summer's day. The space in your universe is fertile beyond our telling, although your astronomers can perceive some of its open ended expansion these days as computers make their observational and computational tasks easier. Here, then, among the stars, lie your origin and heritage.

From the Omniverse now, as we approach closer to your own 12th Universe and down to that little Milky Way galaxy which seems so immense to you, there are several areas and constellations nearby that have historical and present relationships with Earth. I mention particularly the delightful "Seven Sisters"—the Pleiades—the constellation of Orion, and also the beautiful star, Sirius, because some souls living on these places once decided to become caretakers of C-ton when it needed assistance.

Because these particular stars and areas have some of their soul seeds upon your planet even yet, they will be gently lifting that veiled remembrance in the coming years through energy signals.

Eighty percent of the 11 million souls who originally immigrated as caretakers to C-ton came from those places just mentioned. The Pleiades, the largest single source, was joined by others from constellation Orion, some from Sirius, and a few volunteers from scattered, less known planets in this, and other, universes.

These souls who started the Earth's development looked a little different *then* than you do now. Pleiadeans, especially, had some physical denseness with a roundness of head and body style similar to yours today, but their bodies were more uniformly the same.

On Earth you have a book about the Pleiadeans with huge beautiful colored illustrations in which these beings from a UFO appear to look just like you, but this is primarily a projection because they want you to accept them on first contact. Then, as you become used to their method of telepathic communication and are "easy" with their energy, they cease the illusion they are presenting and let you gradually perceive their real appearance. By this time you have built up a harmonious friendship and you therefore respond favorably. Perhaps you become aware of a slight change, but by now you are communicating on a friendship frequency, so you do not perceive a profound difference. Can you understand this? In the film called <u>E.T.</u> the child truly loves another being whose physical body is not "human."

Nonetheless, due to your violent natures on Earth, when you have been contacted by intergalactic beings, for safety reasons, they often present the idea and/or picture that they are *not* dif-

135

ferent. Yes, you have had presentations of smaller, different energies, but then your artists also draw beings that appear to have a beautiful human countenance. If you line up those beautiful drawings and observe them, they almost look alike. Why? Because this is a picture being projected to prevent fear and attack. Would you not also wish to protect yourself in potentially unsafe places? Many of those smaller beings are the truer forms, while the ones that look similar to you are probably projections.

Right now on Earth when a human is a little bit different there is usually a fear or revulsion factor. If someone has a distorted countenance, and yet their heart is pure, you still pull back. The intergalactic, or stellar beings, know how the human reacts to something that is considered "different," and so they try not to upset you. You seem to go for that which is physically appealing, seeing the outside countenance first, not the heart or soul's intention. You are still trapped by the illusion of the physical world where that which is beautiful is merely a personal discernment of each individual.

These energy lifeforms who live in other places in your own galaxy are able to easily associate with each other in an accepted way through the intellect and telepathic communication. They work with true understanding of energy frequencies. That which is seen as the physical container is not the reality.

Someday, by raising your energy frequencies, you will expand parts of the human brain that are not presently in use. In the future you will need those additional brain regions where certain electrical impulses and frequency capabilities reside so you can communicate with other lifeforms. When you are contacted by beings who use a different frequency than yours, wouldn't it be exciting to have telepathic understanding? Even now on Earth you have blind people who are using this frequency method already; they are using their sensors, which are

136

not being distorted by visual receptivities. They are working with *vibrations*. In your future, humans will use energy vibrations for many things.

But for several years your contact with stellar beings—*stellar* means the ability to travel anywhere within space—might best be put in abeyance until there is a higher level of spiritual awareness. As the spiritual awareness increases, the *receptivity* to that which is different will increase. The differences will be lessened because your attunement will be higher. This acceptance will carry over to those with different skin colors, nationalities, and so on—for we are working to unite everyone and lessen all prejudices.

Greater acceptance in areas such as politics, social consciousness, economics, and health is going to break down old customs and unloving beliefs. Climatic changes may affect many and aid in unifying you into what is called "brotherhood." This year is already beginning the shift. Within the next two years there will be further elimination of separative attitudes.

It is possible, too, that galactic inhabitants such as the Pleiadeans might contact those former associates who wish it by using energy beams to stimulate development of a keener receptivity and an eagerness to work together for success of peace on Earth.

The question has been asked of us, "During the prior time of difficulty on Earth roughly 7 million years ago when the Rebel Ray caused the separation, did these other lifeforms, whose immigrant friends had come to Earth, have any desire to help?"

The answer to that is—there was no way they could help then. However, there is great concern now that such an event never happen again. You see, the ones who left and came here were under an agreement or contract that they would continue their work until it was finished. Thus, they became part of the new planet's population, and there was not to be interference from the former place. What was perceived by the ones who remained on the Pleiades was that their friends had left on a longterm adventure. They knew the emigrants were involved in something that was exciting for them, something new, so they wished them well. No one in our realms perceived any great difficulty occurring; consequently, there was no plan of emergency action set up by the Pleiadeans and other home ports or us.

Now we often get questions about your galactic cousins and their procreative patterns. Be assured they are not sexually interested in you, nor do they have the same procreative method. They seldom have children and only if the offspring is truly needed and wanted.

There should be *no fear* of any type of improper physical advance from the Pleiadeans, for they are peace loving and would not wish to overpower. They would not necessarily find your ways attractive, in any case. Your lower physical vibrations cause even your own solar system lifeforms to talk about the "energy stench" of the auras emitted by most Earth dwellers.

It is important, also, to remember that you probably would have more consideration from these higher lifeforms than from many of your own Earth mates—due to their social structure—though we hope this will soon change. The majority of Pleiadean energies are in caring or bonding situations. They tend to have communal relationships with groups of people in size from six, eight, ten, twelve, twenty-four; even larger groups. They live together, male and female energies, not segregated.

They are not aware of time in their dimension and do not have the same political and economic problems you have here on your planet. So when I tell you they work with research and medical or planetary concerns such as astronomy and movements of the planets, understand they are not "stressed out." Their life interests are at a level that is slower than yours and that is for the betterment of, and service to, all. They do not have the same concerns that you have on your planet because they have no warfare. Do you recognize that warfare is the main occupation upon this planet? If you were to step back and truly look at the primary activities on your planet, your score on negativity, violence, and war would be very high.

You have a little Earth saying: "Would some gift the Gods would give us to see ourselves as others see us."

Earth souls, we are giving you that gift now.

I ask, finally, that you look back at the illustration of the Omniverse. In it, please notice that the twelve universes are depicted as enclosed "bodies" with defined structure. This is inaccurate scientifically, but we use it to show that even the great vastness of space has regions that, though expanding, are somewhat defined to avoid catastrophic collision. Since we did not include beautiful color photographs of the universe, please go look at the highly recommended astronomy books in your library just for the thrilling joy of the pictures! Astronomy is changing rapidly—not only for learning what is out there—but for learning what is inside of you in relation to us. Then learn what you can astronomically and combine this with what you call quantum or advanced physics. Here are answers for both the mind and the heart. Here are answers for the soul.

We wish you could see life as we do, for when we look out over the Omniverse we see light, sparkling bright with color, vibrant in its vitality and always seeking continuance of existence and creative expression. Worlds beyond worlds—how can we describe them all? And you are part of it.

When you can feel the vastness of these tremendous universal firmaments in your thoughts and even in your cells, you will know the joy and glory we have. But when you sense the underlying rhythm that bespeaks a great intelligence's desire to create and cradle its cosmic offspring, you will have the greatest gift of all. You will know peace.

Chapter IX

Evolution and You

Much argument is made on your planet about human species evolving upward out of the apes, gorillas and such. Many of your people believe in this evolutionary process, even as others insist humans are God's direct creation. Your anthropologists are constantly struggling with evidence of something called Neanderthal man and the sudden appearance of a more refined lifeform, the Cromagnon man, with no apparent link between them. Yet you search for that "missing link" most avidly. Since you seek explanation of your evolution as a *physical* structure, let me set the record straight for all who will listen.

Possibly 7.25 million to 7 million years ago, a separate physical creation called human was designed by the Silver Ray and the Supreme Council. Your physical body was created by high spiritual energies.

A human is unique in all of his or her total aspects and did not evolve from something else. We did use the same carbon-based material in later animal forms—those from Uranus especially, which we adapted for Earth. These creations you call apes were brought here some years after humans existed so that there would be a relationship between humans and these other forms. We desired that humans not be arrogant and egotisti-

141

cal—that they not be separate from the planet or animal forms. We wished for humans to keep a symbiotic relationship with all lifeforms.

You tend to interpret your evidence about humans and apes in a backward fashion by insisting apes came first, and humans evolved from them. This is not so. *The rule of creation on your planet is: each species is unique but capable of adaptation.* Humans came first, then the apes, but neither evolved from the other!

You must identify and clear up a genuine confusion about evolution, or you will never understand who you are and what is happening on this planet. Briefly stated, you have two levels of evolution: one that involves the physical body and one that involves your soul. The greater evolution affects body and soul as a unit. Unless you perceive the events of Earth with wisdom, your conclusions about evolution remain illogical. Therefore, in a strange way, both "camps" of argument about evolution's meaning have something to learn.

Those called the creationists, who believe God created them in one quick event without any past or present changes, are in error because we are even now instituting changes to improve both the physical body and the soul. By the same token, those who think that humans came from apes need to grasp that we first created human bodies as a container for the soul and imported apes as companions thereafter.

This clarification could lead to a greater unity on your planet about who you are and where you are situated on the pathway back to God.

Let us briefly review what we have told you about human bodies or that which you call physical life, as background for everyone. The body came nearly one million years after the souls were hovering over Earth in their glowing spiritualized energy rays. Bodies were a "rescue package" that we created specifically to keep the souls from diminishing further. *The body did not come first.* It would never have been created, in fact, if the spiritual separation had not occurred.

This physical body was a gift to help the diminishing souls and was nearly perfect as a temporary housing unit. Your bodies once lasted thousands of years; they were self-healing and easily repairable. They also allowed some soul activity outside the body's confines during sleep or rest periods.

Although we created this wonderful physical machine for your soul's temporary residence, the Rebel Ray's negative frequency influence distorted some of those near-perfect models and reduced their structures to a pitifully primitive state called cave man. We are still working to improve all bodies for you of Earth so you can regain the positive features originally available in your body machine.

Part of this reparation is happening now as we bring high energy vibrations to the planet, and our intermediate goal of giving information about the body machine design and function should soon start to balance and extend human life. We would like to increase your age span to at least an average of 90 years and then 125 years by the Time of Radiance. About midterm in those happy years, a lifespan of at least 500 years should be possible, especially as your healers begin to use colors to treat disease and injury, along with other new treatments based on understanding the body as fueled by energy.

You have a part to play in this reparation by cleaning up your planetary home, establishing peace, and preserving the air, water, and other essentials. We are inspiring inventors to create more solar, wind, and other "clean" energy resource applications and are also trying to channel ideas for new types of homes so that you work and live in attunement with the natural environment. Ideas about wearing materials that are lightweight, adaptable to weather variations, and yet non-polluting and disposable—unlike some of your present plastic-based garments—should soon be manifested.

We have mentioned food applications from the oceans to allow the cells more pure energy vitality, which in turn creates keener mental perception and greater physical health.

As your cells increase their energy vibrations and vitality, and the brain opens parts of its long-forgotten capabilities, you may speak once again to the animals—and each other—telepathically. You will be in tune with the stars and eventually all of the universe, of creation itself, as this body is reclaimed as an ingenious vehicle for your soul's journey.

So we wish to assure you that the physical body was nearly perfect, but has fallen into a very weakened condition. It is receiving our attention even as our soul reclamation project brings you home from that lower, dense physical estate.

Sometimes people of Earth will ask how we are helping their soul evolve if God created it perfect in the first place, and this is a very basic, welcome question.

When the Silver Ray brought forth your seven-foot energy ray you were without a physical body, and unless that energy were adversely affected—by negative sound frequency, for example—it would be eternal. However, please remember the information we have shared. The souls were affected by sound frequencies and did lose their illumination, size, and vitality, whereupon our mission of soul salvation began. It is like having a million dollars in the bank, and then somebody swindles most of it away from you—you no longer have the full amount. Likewise, your soul's energy rate and level were taken away, and you consequently have less of it than you did. This kind of evolution, to regain that which was lost, is actually restitution. You are regaining the intelligence of the soul itself—its former purity and cosmic or divine qualities.

While living on Earth's present low awareness level, you

are regaining your reverence for God and the higher forces, and you are taking responsibility for your caretaker's role in the planet's evolutionary phase to regain its fallen estate. We often speak about this topic, but it is absolutely critical! When your vibrations dimmed, you lost remembrance of your origin and cosmic relationships. Your present evolutionary progress should bring that remembrance clearly back in focus to a high all-knowing state. Like a gradual transfusion, your true essence is being restored even while living in a physical body in a dense vibrational world.

To explain this in simple terms, you are becoming brighter, lighter, and more loving. You were reduced to a mere candle flame, but a greater blaze of light, once yours, is being restored.

Now, one of your major tools for understanding evolution—be it spiritual or physical—is to open your mind to new ideas about what you call "evidence." It is also necessary to accept that your original identity is that of a *soul*, which is an actual beam of energy. You are light.

A blind man who touches only the tip of your nose would have a difficult time describing a human face if asked to do so with only that evidence. Then consider that bits of bone, partial skeletons, and other materials—the so-called evidence to explain evolution—could lead you astray since you look to the physical body for proof without knowing its relationship to the soul. Yet we applaud your curiosity, interest, and desire to know who you are and what your species has been doing on the planet.

Please ponder what is now said, as I review the setting and circumstances that caused what your holy writings call "the fall". You have not had a complete explanation before now.

Do you remember that 11 million souls, each a seven-foot-high vertical ray of energy, but without a physical body like yours, immigrated to become caretakers of an experimental station at the outer regions of the then known universe?

Yes, they left their homes in the Pleiades, Orion, Sirius, and other such established galactic population centers to be caretakers of a beautiful new planet, C-ton. They were to be cocreators in developing the plant species, even some animals, until these could be successfully nurtured. These souls contracted to stay on C-ton until their job was *finished*, however long that took, and all were given *free will* to enjoy the vast variety that would be part of this planet's uniqueness.

Not only were they to enjoy this new adventure on a spectacular planet of rare beauty and abundant variety, but they were to retain a caring for the planet itself and for the great First Cause of all life even though separated from their own origins where spiritual commitment was high.

These scientific space pioneers then began their work under Archangel Michael's aegis and generally enjoyed their great adventure for approximately 800,000 years before that encounter with the Rebel Ray. This event changed the planet's destiny and brought the caretakers' soul light to near extinction.

As you learn, today, about "the fall," please realize that the continuing cycle of destruction on Earth has brought the Great Rays here now with intention to heal your souls. We intend to cleanse and restore the planet. We intend to bring the Time of Radiance with its joy, beauty, and glory, to all who will honor God and live peacefully.

Now, before "the fall" occurred and while Archangel Michael was away on galactic business, a few of C-ton's staff had expressed dissatisfaction with their long adventure. Thus, when the one called Rebel Ray sent his energy beam to cause dissension among the souls with intention to overtake the planet, he expected to compromise their reverence for God and

146

transfer it to his own personal glory.

In his original attempts, using an intellectual argument to win the caretakers' reverence for himself, he was thwarted. The majority of the group continued to face the northerly direction to energize themselves with God's cosmic energy.

Failing in that task, the Rebel Ray began what you would call a radio broadcast of intellectual argument and sound frequency disturbances. The caretakers first noticed a change in animal behavior. Some animals became vicious and cannibalistic. Although vegetarian by creation, a few animals now murdered each other. Still the souls, themselves, did not perceive great danger, or they would have communicated with Lord Michael for assistance.

As the sound frequency disturbances continued, however, many souls suddenly succumbed to this powerful bombardment. Almost before the expedition knew what had happened and could call to Archangel Michael to return with help, irreparable damage had occurred. Souls became confused and behaved irrationally. In brief, many turned away from the northern flow of God's cosmic energy whereupon their soul rays were even more adversely affected. The souls shrank in size; their light essence dimmed. Tragedy loomed dangerously near.

By the time Archangel Michael could bring the Blue Ray energy to protect the shrinking souls, the expedition was in total chaos. The great battle spoken of in your scriptures between the light and the dark was lost by the holy light forces. Although courageous in the face of serious difficulties, Michael, master of the Blue Ray, did not prevail over the Rebel Ray, and C-ton fell under that beings's influence.

There was mayhem after the Rebel Ray's victory. Souls were confused. They now knew pain and sorrow; they felt bereft of those they trusted. We regret the details of such an event, but they are necessary background for your complete understanding of human evolution.

The souls then became "endangered" because their light was actually shrinking and dimming under the continuing negativity of the Rebel Ray's vibrational contact.

The Great Rays were disturbed at these events and wished to make a positive effort lest the souls be totally lost. A novel plan was quickly devised and offered as a temporary escape which would lead back into the higher realms at a later time.

What happened then? The Silver Ray and the Supreme Council created a container called the human body to house the expiring soul. Frankly, this body was a magnificent model, as you may agree, and many rapidly dimming souls chose to enter these forms to save their light and one day evolve back to prior brilliance. Thus came "the fall" spoken of in written scriptures. The souls were small and dim now, but they had a temporary sanctuary.

Are you wondering how the details of our "rescue plan for souls" worked? Quickly, before the Rebel Ray could interfere, Archangel Michael and other spiritual beings came to explain the dilemma and all souls were told that their safety and continuance could not be guaranteed unless they chose residence within a physical body with entrance through the top of the head. (You still have a place there for soul access that is quite soft and vulnerable.)

Thus began an evolutionary cycle with souls living in matter still under the Rebel Ray's focused influence. Now you have never understood this next part, so we share the facts for your anthropological study.

Some of the souls now living in physical bodies were able to resist that dark one's influence through free will choice by continuing to seek God's cosmic energy. Others did not. The ones who did not, eventually became bentover, stooped down, and depressed in the head and brain, causing diminished intellectual capacity. It eventually became impossible for them to raise themselves up into a truly vertical position and look out and above toward God.

These heavy bodied humans you find skeletons of were examples of our first creation that, over time, lost their erectness and beauty under the negative influence of the Rebel Ray's frequency bombardment.

Thus, the cave man was caused by reducing our superbly erect, magnificent physical body to nearly a beast form, even while other bodies withstood the Rebel Ray's control and maintained our original pattern of vertical prowess and intelligence.

Interesting, is it not, that the two forms—one under the influence of the Rebel Ray and another still revering God—continued life on the same planet simultaneously? Your history does not show that these two civilizations were parallel, but you may be assured they did exist at the same time! Not all of your human life was bent over in what you call "prehistoric" times.

The great library destroyed in Alexandria had a full history of the progression of souls living in human bodies upon Earth, and there are still a few hidden documents scattered in unknown depositories. Most records are buried under miles of upchurned earth or far under water, however, lost to those who seek.

In seeing these grotesque human forms you misunderstand what has happened and assume a faulty evolutionary explanation. Souls entered physical bodies, some of which became distorted and existed simultaneously. Later we brought the adapted ape family and other domestic type animal forms since there were but a few small creatures on Earth then. We wonder if you can fathom this data?

149

In the continuing struggle to save the souls, now encased in physical bodies, we used several plans to extricate them, but this was seen as ineffective after many years. Too much ground was lost. Because the souls got used to the excitement of bodily experimentation, their entire being changed, and they began to adapt to the planet.

Male and female energies had been made for continuance of life and mutual companionship, but never since "the fall" has humanity ever used the full potential of the body container as it was first made. Still, your body is an ideal vehicle for the soul because high attunement to God is inherent in its design.

As humanity continued in its miserable, fallen estate, only sleep, dreams, and death became our aids in this great soul restitution program. Although sleep was designed to help the body cleanse itself daily and restore its physical machinery, it also provides the time of remembering. It is a special time—different even than conscious meditation—when a soul can recall its real, or spiritual, existence.

This sleep process was accomplished by putting in an invisible body clock—or what you call "biorhythm"—that would require the body to sleep. It is controlled by the Sun, Moon, and the gravitational pull. These affect the liquid in the body so it must rest.

In the early years, when souls first entered into physical bodies, a soul could consciously leave and return while the body slept. It could only go a short distance, however, since we had not yet created a silver cord of energy. This nightly excursion of popping in and out helped souls retain remembrance of God and their own true nature as light.

Regrettably, even sleeping finally became a mere physical experience for most humans, and before long they totally forgot who they were. Dreams, visions, and contemplative messages were retained but stayed mainly on the periphery of life as almost mysterious things.

Although the Gold Ray, now designated as the Christ Light, sent its supportive energy beam around the planet for encouragement and support to counterbalance the Rebel Rays's control, those souls seemed trapped by their dense physical surroundings. Just a few were able to remember God and use the Christ Light to achieve personal enlightenment.

Since the entire original group had contracted to be caretakers of the planet and was attempting to return to that capacity, those who did free themselves from bondage became Earth's spiritual teachers and tried to guide the languishing diminished souls. But little progress occurred.

In the early times the physical body creations we gave you lasted thousands of years, so if the soul's opportunity to remember God while embodied on Earth was wasted, there was little prospect for spiritual advancement. Our rescue ratio was so poor that another plan was finally instituted to outwit and outweigh the Rebel Ray's influence. Because the universal law of cause and effect had placed souls in serious imbalance by their negative actions, we created the plan of repetitive experience. In your world you call this reincarnation. Its object was to allow a soul to have cumulative learning and growth opportunities rather than be limited by long lives foolishly spent with little chance to correct former mistakes.

Only at physical death could the now very small soul finally be allowed full freedom to remember its origins. There, in the heavenly realms, it would review its negative Earth life with disbelief and return to a body committed to honor God and all of life.

This repetitive experience plan meant shorter physical life periods, so by now some souls had acquired hundreds (sometimes thousands) of these Earth trips. Because many souls continued to forget love and peace during each visit, they gathered so much negative behavior, or karma, that their souls seemed doomed. On Earth they were caught up in war, pillage, rape, and violence that threatened all life and prevented peace. Ignorant and unloving, souls played dreary, hateful games, seeking power and control over one another. Your history reeks with such activities! And many more of the worst events are hardly known, even so.

Yet within all this ignorance great teachers and enlightened ones persistently brought the truth and promise of redemption. And among the nations, large and small, their voice for God was spoken, recorded, and modeled as encouragement to the still-sleeping ones.

Throughout this 7-million-year negative experience the holy light forces would sometimes intensify the ray energies to counteract and overcome the Rebel Ray's influence and prevailing conditions. During these times, your history records what you call a renaissance, or bursting forth of truth, light, knowledge, and beauty. Irregular though these periods were, they have been essential in the souls' growth toward love, peaceful behavior, and caring for each other and the planet. Then be glad of these cosmic leaps when our energies have fueled your advancement to the next level. These consciousness expansions are not your creation, per se, but the additional energy we bring has allowed you to use these high vibrations to great advantage.

In evolution, then, your quantum movements have been based on our intensified spiritual support. You have the greatest of these energy supports on your planet now so your soul, within its human body, can attune to the God force energy and the Great Rays' present amplification. It is your willingness to receive and correctly use these higher vibrations that makes this pregnant Time of Awakening so fruitful.

Please understand that in creation certain aspects are set in motion and left to brew a while. This "brewing" is part of evolution from our point of view. Therefore, we see no "missing links" that you seek. After we plant soul seeds, or instigate certain life processes, there is a germination time; that is all. If you study history you can see some of the obvious ones.

Because humanity's soul progress rate continues to lag, our commitment is to bring about a *rapid* change, so that all peoples in all the lands on Earth can receive amplification of spiritual energies *immediately and simultaneously.* Having small centers of light scattered within various nations has not brought the planet peace nor the souls permanent joy. Therefore, we firmly progress into the most fantastic plan ever coordinated in your universe.

Evolution for you and the planet is now so speeded up that your time seems to evaporate. We Rays are personally in charge of evolutionary progress for both the dense physical body and soul creations. Rejoice that your soul mastery looms nearer with every breath because of our intervention. The energy vibrations we bring increase your soul's opportunity for evolution by a rapid acceleration margin. Again we say rejoice! For any former negative actions of your many lives will now be cancelled if you choose to acknowledge your soul's purpose, preserve all life, and seek only peace. Whatever the soul blemishes may be, they can all be forgiven!

Now, one of the most difficult barriers to your spiritual evolution concerns that which is called your scriptures, bibles, and other holy material—the books, legends, and stories of past times. They are to help you but not to limit your present advancement. Many on Earth today have become extremely self-righteous and divided from other believers by narrow views and interests. Rather than drawing closer to establish peace, these separate factions are multiplying and creating divisions among groups we expected to bond in unity.

In one way, these spiritual materials are your greatest friends, for they speak of beautiful moral values and give uplifting examples and models of how love and peace should be used as the primary standards of life. Yet most of these holy books are only guidelines and adaptations of previously stated ideas that help you reach higher truths. The greatest prophets reiterated the message of God's plan for love and peace, but they also gave *current* information *for the people of that time* and for a specific culture's or group's benefit.

Thus the one called Moses delivered a message as well as suggesting an action. Who but an Archangel delivered the Koran to the Middle Eastern people who asked for guidance for positive action?

It was the contemplative Buddha, listening within the quiet whispering of his soul to even greater guides, who brought a design for living action. It was Krishna who followed an inner voice from God and outlined a plan for action with many pathways to God.

It is well known that Jesus spoke for love and peace and especially urged the healing action of forgiveness. So all great truths explain that any guiding principle should be expressed by action. *Evolution is based upon principle put into action.* This action leads to higher purpose and expressed behavior or it is valueless. Therefore, although evolution is a continuum, it is also a blossoming of spring after fallow times of rest. It has its own seasons, but *we* are evolution's architects.

Some humans have difficulty accepting that the creators are in charge of the evolutionary process, even though a species can have its own adaptation. They do not like assigned roles such as humanity has, but we ask you to accept your role and fulfill its purpose. Also recognize that life is evolving. Other planets and beings in your solar system are evolving; galactic neighbors and their habitations are also evolving as physical matter, lifeforms, and light forms. Thus you are not evolving as a unit apart from all the rest. You live, grow, and evolve *together*.

Evolution is removing past barriers and restrictions so that new movement is possible. Have you thought of it that way? Evolution is growth or forward movement followed by a period of rest and evaluation. If error has occurred, it must be corrected so that new energy can bring about the next phase of expansion. By this cosmic link of events evolution brings you into the higher dimensions of consciousness. Yes, there is physical expression of the species, but it is the soul evolution that best expresses God.

As these next years advance, each aspect of human existence, whether individual, family, group, political, business, economic, educational, and so on, will go through changes that are a form of evolution, or progress.

All that is created is involved in some form of evolution, which is also termed *change* or *progress*. You notice that the word progress is emphasized, especially for those of Earth who have already experienced the reverse of it—regression.

The Time of Awakening is to allow you this wonderful soul alignment with cosmic purpose. This re-alignment with the vitality of soul expansion, progress, or evolution of life itself, is pure aliveness. So that you can feel *true life*, the actual vitality of cosmic energy, we are charging your planet with more radiance and illumination than you can imagine.

The season we bring you now is that spurt of quickened growth your heart has sobbed for in its darkest hours. But to gain this advancement of soul cleansing, we ask you for one vital gift. Use the energy we give for positive, present day action. Yes, honor the truth of God's power and presence as the Creator of all life—wherever you hear it and from whichever religion or philosophy it comes. This truth is the constant, unfailing certainty to build your life upon. But also listen for those *updated* messages or increased awarenesses that will serve humanity's current plan and next movement back to God. Today you are being asked to consider this message for those same two aspects: its expression of love and caring for God and its current information to help you grasp the meaning of *today's* events.

The main principle of evolution we use is that the species shall be *improved* or refined by the changes that occur. The changes need not be negative, aimless, or unfocused. Because we are now providing the energy impetus you need, evolution will be rapid for a while, even as we have assisted previous civilizations. We propose that you focus on the present and not dwell in the past, for those times and places have already had their own growth opportunities. Yet hopefully you are appreciative about that which has paved your way.

Be grateful for the great civilizations, some of which were probably part of your own former lives, such as Lemuria, Atlantis, Egypt, and ancient regions in the Himalayas or Peru. Cultures in every remaining continent left you messages regarding peace and human relationships of some kind, whether they were called Mayans, Africans, Chinese, Russians, Australians, Hopi, or people of your own Ohio area. The continents of Lemuria and Atlantis are deep beneath the seas, of course, but they left their own legacy with which you presently cope.

We are always hopeful you will be open minded about former civilizations and view them as what you call "object lessons." They had their turn in evolution's cycle. However, it is now *your* turn to learn and grow in this latest chapter of your soul's return to enlightenment, and you are not to be limited by what has gone before—whatever it may have been. There is so much Earth history you don't know that some of it must gradually be revealed to prepare you for a greater galactic role.

For example, when the ancient continent of Lemuria went to her ocean grave in the South Pacific due to Earth changes, outer space beings came to the rescue and moved some of the populace to Peru, a few to North America, Scandinavia, and even Egypt ... not all to one locale. So remnants began anew where they were taken. Such facts explain many mysteries for those who are willing to learn. Since your scientists are too skeptical to explain various human race migrations by anything other than self-propulsion travel by foot or boats, truth remains hidden. Perhaps one day they will finally accept that air travel and rescue by intergalactic spaceships has happened right here on Earth. Your planet is more than the limited place they have defined her to be, and you can be imaginative, courageous, and universal in your thinking. Why shouldn't there be space life watching Earth? Why isn't it possible they fly airships and visit C-ton—then and now? Who says you are isolated in space?

The uninformed who control your education have little or no understanding of these things, but that will change as we bring the true facts of life—as we release our cosmic revelation for all of humanity to ponder.

As we do our part, will you do yours? Will you become a catalyst for truth? A model of love? A bringer of peace?

We call you to become a pace setter and a beacon of illumination. We ask you to resume your role as a caretaker of this planet.

Your moment of cosmic revelation is here. The jewel of you is being polished and faceted in increasing brilliance according to our spiritual plan. You can become magnificent again; your soul can be healed and purified. The hour is now, and it is critical. You are needed, soul of sweet intention. Will you help?

On Earth there is a linear measurement that you term "time." Where we are, beyond that three dimensional limitation, time does not exist. As we bring you home, out of time, all that has apparently happened will be resolved for each soul. Then be happy that the Time of Awakening is here! The negative things of time shall pass away for you as if but a dream, and the sunrise of God's cosmic creation shall redeem the past and maintain the eternal victory of love for all future tomorrows.

It is so.

Aum and Amen.

ADDENDUM

Planetary Commandments

Do you presently belong to some church or organized religion or hold a spiritual belief of some kind? If so, does it begin by teaching you that you are a citizen of a solar system, galaxy, and Universe that has prescribed laws of behavior? If it does, you are indeed blessed and far ahead of your time. Most humans cannot stretch that far yet and have difficulty in loving and respecting even their immediate neighbors on Earth.

You, whose teachers of the past have given instructions regarding proper conduct for the attainment of personal and global peace, are now asked to take a giant step forward as a New Age group. Whether you follow the Ten Commandments, a noble path, a spiritual journey toward bliss, loving God and your human family as yourself, or merely live with demonstrated integrity—you are all called to join in this Time of Awakening as *dwellers of cosmic heritage living under planetary commandments or universal laws.*

Some will say these few commandments we give are merely common sense. This is true. But living them, while you are with free will personality limitations, will take genuine commitment, courage, and caring. Nonetheless, these qualities are inherent within you, and this day we call them forth in their innocence and purity.

The stage is now set for an exciting and miraculous opportunity. But each of you is truly needed to make its unfoldment as smooth as possible. You have an earth code of moral values already. Now practice these recommendations to help yourself become a true citizen of Earth, a caretaker of this battered but beloved garden.

PLANETARY COMMANDMENTS

It is time for you to relate to all that is and to be in harmony with all.

1.   Revere the God force in all things.

2.   Honor the Universe and all created matter in it.

3.   Honor and respect *all* lifeforms—not just human—here and beyond Earth.

4.   Honor your physical planet.

5.   Honor the space around your planet and beyond.

6.   Put no destructive devices in space.

LOVE CORPS NETWORKING

Creating peace on our planet requires commitment and cooperation. If your soul has been touched or your life goals clarified by this book, perhaps you would like to share its message with friends and acquaintances ... give copies for gifts ... write letters to the editors of newspapers, magazines, etc. about peace ... seek peace publicity on radio and TV stations ... have a fundraising event to support such endeavors ... form a local Love Corps group to meditate weekly ... generally help raise humanity's consciousness about the preservation of all life on earth. The Love Corps is an alliance of all human beings who want planetary peace above all else and will work with others to achieve it.

The vital thing for each of us is to meditate daily and also in a weekly group so that we will always have God's presence guiding our daily lives. If you are new to meditation and need temporary support while developing your own inner guidance, we have been asked by The Christ energy to provide a monthly newsletter. It will include answers to reader-submitted questions about the book's concepts and will give any critical messages needed by Love Corps volunteers of all ages during the Time of Awakening.

A Love Corps team will be traveling around the United States to link energies, to share additional information not included in the New Teachings, Secret Truths, and Cosmic Revelation books, and to encourage humanity's achievement of peace and the preservation of all life upon planet earth. If you would like to be involved in the Love Corps endeavors, to participate with us in seminars, or to have individual soul readings, please write to us so we can include your area in our itinerary.

PARTICIPATION QUESTIONNAIRE
AND ORDER FORM

To: SPIRITUAL EDUCATION ENDEAVORS (S.E.E)*
        1556 Halford Avenue, #288
        Santa Clara, CA 95051 USA

Having read <u>Cosmic Revelation,</u> I want to participate in spreading its message. The way I choose to do this is indicated below.

Here's my gift to support and/or expand the **LOVE CORPS** efforts.
___$1,000 or more ___$500 ___$250 ___$100 Other $____
(For tax-deductible contribution, make check payable to The Share Foundation*)

I wish to donate my skills and/or time for: ___Secretarial/Clerical
___Fundraising ___Graphic Arts Design ___Publicity ___Bookkeeping &/or Accounting ___Public Speaking
____Word Processing ____Translating _____Other

I have the following equipment & technical know-how:
____Personal Computer, Make/Model_____
____CB Radio   ____Ham radio equipment

Please send information on how I can help disseminate <u>Cosmic Revelation</u> to:
____Friends, Bookstores, Churches, and Organizations
____Other countries

I would like to help publicize <u>Cosmic Revelation:</u>
___On Radio ___On TV ___In Newspapers/Magazines
___Other (Specify)_____

I would like to be a networker or contact person for the **LOVE CORPS** in my area.____

Check if holding meditation group others may attend.____

(Continued on reverse)

Please send me the monthly Love Corps Newsletter:

_____A 12 month subscription for <u>1987</u> is $30 $_____

or at $3 per issue — circle month (s) desired
J F M A M J J A S O N D $_____
(Foreign 12 month subscription is $40 <u>airmail</u>.
Single issues $4 each.) US dollars <u>only.</u> $_____
Inquire about <u>1988</u> and later subscriptions.

Please send me additional copies of:
<u>Cosmic Revelation</u>:
    Quantity_____@ $9.95 per copy $_____

I wish to order _____copies of <u>New Teachings for</u>
<u>an Awakening Humanity</u> @ $8.95 per copy $_____

I wish to order ___copies of <u>Secret Truths for Teens</u>
<u>& Twenties</u> @ $7.95 per copy $_____

    Minus discount if applicable (see below)** $_____
    Plus 6.5% sales tax (for California residents
      only) $_____
    Plus shipping for 1 book (in U.S. only)*** $ 1.60
    Plus $.70 shipping for each additional book $_____
    to the same address
              Total for books $_____

    TOTAL ENCLOSED $_____

Please <u>Print</u>
Name_____

Address_____

City/State/Zip_____

Phone (optional) (_____)_____

* The Share Foundation (Fed. EIN 94-2699567)
**Love Corps Volunteer discounts:
        5-9 books @ 10% off plus shipping
        10 or more books @ 20% off plus shipping
***Please request foreign shipping rates.

A BOLD, URGENT & EXTRAORDINARY MESSAGE...

"I come to advise you that humanity is not alone in this Universe... that your earth is now being raised back into the higher love dimension she once held... and only those humans who choose peace will be co-creators in this cosmic process.

Time is critical. YOU are needed. Will you help?"
THE CHRIST

...*"This book represents a Communication of the highest order, showing the Path to self-mastery, and providing Divine Insights into God's Plan for the New Golden Age."*

John Randolph Price — Author of The Superbeings, The Planetary Commission, Practical Spirituality; and President of the Quartus Foundation.

...*"It is a truly important work and I know it will be used and appreciated by many folk. I, myself, am glad to add it to my library."*

Judith Skutch Whitson — President, Foundation for Inner Peace, publishers of A Course in Miracles

In *NEW TEACHINGS FOR AN AWAKENING HUMANITY*, the World Teacher takes readers on a spiritual journey of cosmic dimensions from our past, through the present and into the future. In the pages of this book He:

- Clarifies the mission of Jesus 2,000 years ago.

- Challenges the churches to re-evaluate their methods and their role in leading their members to God.

- Outlines a simple meditative program which can enable each of us to restore our links to the higher realms.

- Confronts our scientists and governments with their responsibility in use of scientific discoveries and space weaponry.

- Reminds us that we are the caretakers of our planet and all the life forms on it.

- Emphasizes the high calling of parents and teachers in caring for and teaching the children entrusted to them.

- Provides a glimpse of the wondrous future on earth which awaits us.

- Challenges us to acknowledge our Creator and take action to establish personal and global peace.

Spiritual Education Endeavors Publishing Company
1556 Halford Avenue, #288 • Santa Clara, CA 95051

$8.95 paperback • 5½ x 8½ • 208 pages • ISBN 0-937147-00-1 • Library of Congress Catalog Number: 86-60496

NOTES

NOTES